W0009923

the way forward

yung pueblo

Andrews McMeel
PUBLISHING®

Also by yung pueblo

inward

clarity & connection

lighter

contents

be honest with yourself
about where you are going

how you want to feel
while you are heading there

and who you want to be
when you arrive

every moment is a destination,
an opening, a space for growth

the end goal should not distract you
from taking each step with intention

you are seeing the results of your commitment
and the power of your courage;
the fact that your mind feels *lighter*
shows you that you are moving in the right direction

you are entering into a better life
where your reactions are less intense
and your mind has more flexibility and determination

everything is not perfect;
there are still challenges and times of struggle
but you are learning not to let the down moments define you
and you are more gracefully embracing change

the *inward* journey has sparked your evolution
opened your perspective to a new level of *clarity*
and each *connection* you cherish now has new depth

but the journey is not over
you prepare yourself for another period of growth
with your highest goals in mind and the truth you feel;
your inner wisdom will show you *the way forward*

existing

there are times when all you can do is survive
moments when growing doesn't even seem like an option
and healing feels hundreds of miles away

the trauma and old hurt can weigh so heavily
that all you can do is try to stay afloat,
to endure another day

if existing takes every ounce of your energy,
then that alone is heroic work

people who have revived themselves
after almost drowning in trauma
do not get enough credit

even though the pain
was massive
they did not stay stagnant
or become bitter

they knew the only way out
was the path of healing
and they used it to start a new life

unpopular truth:

what's meant for you will sometimes
feel scary, risky, and new

ease and calm don't always mean
you're moving in the right direction

the biggest rewards usually come
from having the guts and perseverance
to create your own path

i thought the trauma had broken me
but really it gave my life direction

the toxicity made me
embrace communication and honesty

the manipulation made me
realign with my own power

the narcissism showed me
that selflessness is needed

the chaos taught me
to build boundaries

the hurt showed me
that healing and rebirth are possible

the magic happens once you accept
that you can't regulate
others' emotions or experiences

that's when you begin to live
your most authentic life

some people will not "get" you,
but what matters is that *you* get you

be kind,
help others,
and don't forget to live for yourself

it is normal to feel down, tired,
and emotionally exhausted when
you are going through a big transition

especially when you have to let go
of something good for the chance
at something better

great changes are not meant to be easy;
they arise to inspire your growth

maturity is realizing that half of what
you want to say does not need to be said

being able to see the difference
between ego reactions
and helpful points that can uplift harmony
or reaffirm your values
makes a real difference

"speak your truth"
does not mean
"speak your ego"

life will distract you
and pull your senses
in different directions

but within you there is a clear compass
that points relentlessly toward
the freedom you have been seeking

not the unfulfilling freedom of excess
or of being without responsibility

the true freedom that comes from
knowing your mind and body so thoroughly
that wisdom reveals itself to you

embrace the silence
don't fight what arises
accept the waves of change
and let insight unlock truth after truth

until you finally experience undeniable liberation

9 things that hold great power:

rest
kindness
meditation
vulnerability
healing yourself
being honest with others
embracing lifelong growth
fostering deep connections
giving without wanting in return

it is only heavy
because you are deciding
over and over again
to carry it

embrace change,
loosen up your sense of identity,
let yourself walk a new path

you do not have to ignore
or erase the past,
you just have to wholeheartedly
embrace the present and move on

emotional maturity is not about being
above your emotions

it is about being able to sit
with the rawness of every feeling
without letting it take over
your mind and actions

it is about facing storms
without getting blown away

i got lost while trying to survive

my mind was busy fighting itself
my energy was focused on acting as if i were stable
my heart felt clogged up with old pain

the struggle continued until i realized
that dwelling on the past
would never change what happened

slowly my attention shifted to the present
accepting myself gave me back some of my energy

i began to carve a new road
one that would lead to better things

along the way i found
the parts of me that i had misplaced

as i was busy building
a life that supports my peace of mind,
healing gave me a guiding lesson:
to continue moving forward i simply need
to treat myself and others
with gentleness and honesty

love is much bigger than relationships

love is the way you heal yourself,
the kindness you give others,
the gentleness you give yourself in turbulent times,
the space you hold for close friends,
the intention with which you live in the present,
and the energy that changes the world

love is every moment that elevates the human experience
and all the small things that make life shine

manage your reactions
but do not suppress your emotions

even after the love was gone
we hung on to each other

because we wanted to avoid
the sting of heartache
and the hard work
of rebuilding our lives

we let it drag on so long
that time felt stagnant
and colors lost their brightness

the mismatch was evident
the fights were exhausting
patience felt overstretched

until the day came
when it was time to face the hurt

the tears ran freely
the sorrow felt explosive
a major chapter was finally closing

just as a star explodes in grandeur
our parting produced the energy to begin again

it took this great loss
for both of us to eventually feel
fully revitalized

the clearest red flag
is if they are consistently
bringing out the worst in you

the hard truth
is that a connection
doesn't automatically lift you up

sometimes it aggravates
the roughest parts of your old conditioning
and brings things to the surface
in an unhealthy way

when someone doesn't know
how to process their own tension,
they project it onto whoever
is closest to them

it is easier to place the blame on others
than to see yourself clearly

proximity breeds tension
because egos are rough

the friction between egos
ignites unnecessary arguments

don't let the storm limit what you can see. light is bound to appear again, especially because you can change things. these heavy feelings are but a short note in the history of your life. it is easy to forget the depth of your power when everything feels rough. you have already overcome so much to be where you are now. tough moments are common before a great victory.

lean on the fact that you are more than a survivor. you are more than your past. you are more than what hurts. old habits do not define you. you are a hero who is ready to emerge. your transformation will inspire others to do the hard things they need to do to thrive. even if this moment is a struggle, you can always start again.

i used to see my past as a hindrance

all of the mistakes i have made
all of the failed relationships
all of the pain i was given
that i never wanted to carry

at first i wanted to forget these memories
to scratch them out of the book of my life

but now i see that even though my story started heavy,
that did not stop me from finding my inner light

my sadness was a motivator
my pain became my teacher

if you listen closely to your hurt,
it will say "there is a better way than this"

and all you have to do is respond
"show me, i'm ready"

you have to be willing to admit
when you have lost your way

it is normal to lose sight of what's important,
to stumble and take a few steps backward

a long journey is never a straight line

gently telling yourself the hard truth
is the best method for realigning
and getting back on the right path

intention is one of the most powerful
forces in the universe

it sets actions into motion
and gives them a direction

words get their energy from the intention
we place into them

if you want to reclaim your power,
start by being intentional

i want to love everyone without judging them,
without placing anyone on a scale of better or worse

to first see the good in people and
treat them with kindness and attention

i want to give without worrying
about what i will get in return

i want my mind to feel comfortable
radiating love to the entire world

i want to gently hold myself to a higher standard
without forcing or rushing

you know the inner work
is paying off

when you can see your ego
trying to make a mess of things

but you have enough resilience
and awareness

to choose peace instead of chaos

wisdom is when you notice
that your emotions are heavy
and overheated
before other people do

you notice your passive-aggressive tone
when it's starting
or when your choice of words
becomes rougher

this is when you intentionally
slow things down
and treat yourself and others gently
as the inner storm passes

reminder:

it is hard to connect well with other people
when you are feeling exhausted and depleted

when your energy is low,
the mind will want to revert
to performative behavior
that lends itself to superficial interactions

it takes energy to go deep,
to give someone your presence

intentionally disconnecting is powerful

unfollowing,
turning off social,
and not responding to every message
can boost your mental health

you don't always have to be on

unconscious disconnection limits relationships;
intentional disconnection helps you find your center

yung pueblo

next time you think of yourself harshly
or want to force yourself to grow,
remember that the only way
to move forward is organically.

you are nature and nature cannot help
but flow at a genuine and unhurried pace.

if you really want to speed things up,
set goals, walk toward them without attachment,
and peacefully align with actions
that feed your inner harmony.

after the cocoon period, when you are in full bloom,
take advantage of this powerful energy

create what your intuition is asking you to

stay open to new connections

make the moves that will change your life

do the hard things your capacity can handle

live adventurously

if someone close to you
is trying to make you act just like them,
they are not loving you well

thinking that your way is the ideal way
is an ego trap that leads to pushing people away

we are not meant to be the same

to love well is to appreciate
another's approach to life

sometimes we go back
to our old life
for a little while
to remember
that it no longer fits

when you left, it was a shock,
because you told me
we were going to build our lives together

now i'm left with half a plan
a heart that feels torn
and the remnants of memories
i no longer want

success is so subjective
that if you do not develop inner peace,
you can find yourself chasing after it endlessly

success will continue to take on new forms,
each more tantalizing than the last,
always pushing back the finish line

don't let craving make you forget:
you are already whole

feel it all
whatever may come up
even if the present hurts
even if the past is roaring
heroes do not run away
healing is not won easily

feel wisely
without letting what is temporary control you
acceptance makes real freedom possible

old hurt sometimes burns
as it leaves your being

letting go can feel like an illness
that leaves you shaken
without fully knocking you down

the tension that was once deep inside
finally found space to rise to the surface
so that it could evaporate
and no longer weigh on your mind

when the mind is turbulent, it becomes easy to drop logical and sensible thinking. your anxiety and stress can create elaborate fictions in your mind. a strong emotion can attach itself to any little piece of information and build a wild story around it. the mind is quick to rely on imagination to keep the heavy reaction going.

fear and its manifestations push us to overanalyze and place us in unhealthy mental loops that increase our tension. this is common in all human beings. it is a pattern reinforced by our need to evade potential dangers, but if it goes unchecked, it can also burden the mind and create behavioral complexes that make life more difficult.

recognizing what it feels like when you are out of balance can help you cut the loop. awareness is the light that helps break unconscious habit patterns. similarly, training the mind to become comfortable in the present moment will help you have the strength to pull yourself out of imaginary negativity. you must get comfortable with turning your attention inward if you want to start living in a new way. when you become familiar with your own ups and downs, it will be easier to see when you are causing yourself misery.

you need to do more
than eat nourishing food,
exercise, and rest to feel your best

you also need to be around good people,
spend time healing your emotional history,
live in alignment with your values,
say no to people-pleasing,
stay open to growth,
and deeply embrace change

realizing you spoke to someone harshly
because you were agitated
is actually a sign of progress

before you can stop yourself from
saying things you later regret,
you must first notice yourself doing it

self-awareness makes changed behavior possible

your intuition will lead you outside your comfort
zone so that you can grow

confusion comes from being disconnected from your intuition. learning to align with what feels right, not in the sense of following your cravings but in the sense of moving toward what supports your evolution and your highest good, is a necessary skill.

there are two critical things to understand about intuition. the first is that it doesn't care about your comfort zone. it will ask you to be bold and valiant even if you do not feel ready. just like love, intuition is a vehicle for growth. if you listen to it, it will help you reach new personal heights. but to get there, you will have to face what is weighing you down and fully let it go.

the second is that it may ask you to place yourself in difficult situations where you have to face your fears, but it will never ask you to hurt yourself. intuition will invite you to be courageous, but it will not lead you into a reckless dead end.

attuning to your intuition is a personal process. for me, intuition feels like a calm knowing that appears in my body. if i don't listen to it at first, it will reappear sporadically with tranquil certainty. intuition has a softness to it, even when it asks you to make bold moves.

intuition is quite different from the reactive rambles of the mind or moments of emotional upheaval; while reactivity carries tension, intuition flows smoothly and steadily with information that can help you.

4 ways to remain in alignment:

don't listen to the feeling that you need to perform for others

say no to situations that burn way too much of your energy

surround yourself with people who love the authentic you

let your intuition guide you, not your fears or cravings

on feeling

the ability to feel is often seen as a burden combined with a
blessing. it is not only one of the essential mediums that you
use to navigate life and the world but also where your greatest
joys begin and your deepest sorrows take root. heartache and
happiness exist on different ends of the same spectrum of
emotions. how you react to what you feel is often your greatest
source of dissatisfaction and stress. more, your past and
present manifest themselves through your ability to feel. your
conditioning is not just something that is intellectual; it is also
experienced through the sensations you feel in your body. how
you feel often morphs from something that is meant to inform
you into something that dominates the way you think and act.
healing and personal growth are grounded in establishing a
new relationship with what you feel.

the default for many is that they let their feelings make
decisions for them. this does not always yield the best results,
because what you feel often dramatizes the narrative in your
mind and leads you into making big decisions based on
impermanent emotions. when you let your strongest emotions
take center stage, it becomes easy to feed your own tension—
like when you react to your anger with more anger, which
simply makes the tension you feel bigger and bigger. we often
react to strong emotions by forgetting that the ever-present
law of change ensures that what we feel in this moment will
not last forever. a storm may be powerful, but no storm
is endless.

continued

continued

giving space to what you feel is always valuable because it is an essential part of healing and letting go, but if you let it take control, then it will be too easy to fall into past patterns. *being with it is better than becoming it.* there is a subtle space you should become more familiar with, the space where reclaiming your power is truly possible—the space where you can feel a fire burning within you without giving it more fuel.

this spaciousness of mind becomes more available to you when you realize that your first reaction is just your past trying to re-create itself. left unchecked, your reactions will keep you in a loop where you are looking at your present life through the lens of your past emotional history. if you keep giving power to your first impulse, then you will keep reacting the same way you have reacted in your past. this way of living leaves little room for growth and for anything new to emerge.

the challenge you face is building enough self-awareness so that you can actively and repeatedly say no to your past when it wants to take over. saying no to your past doesn't mean suppressing it; it just means that you will let yourself feel whatever has come up, but you make the choice to allow your present self to remain the dominant force.

the days of letting your old fears and anxieties make all the decisions for you are over. a new time has arisen where you are patiently creating room so that your present self can decide what actions will keep you on a path that is truly nourishing and liberating. it is time to let the past rest and fully embrace the present.

your capacity for happiness quietly expands
whenever you let yourself sit with your sorrow.

when darkness no longer scares you,
your mind will be able to perceive more light.

each moment you spend tending to your old wounds
makes space for new peace.

each moment of forgiveness
gives you new direct routes to joy.

when you decide to let yourself feel, unbind, and let go,
you naturally start receiving life with gentler hands.

the quest you take to free your heart from the past
simultaneously elevates your future
and improves your ability to love.

just because you feel a connection with them
does not mean they are right for you

the hard truth is that you need more
than a spark to build a home

attraction is common,
but fitting together
like two pieces of a puzzle
is rare

if something about their energy
feels off or rough,
that's your sign that building with them
may not be the best idea

it's important to be kind
and to help when you can,
but that doesn't mean everyone
has a right to your time

design a rejuvenating space for yourself

it is easy to get lost
in the infinite space of hypotheticals

instead of focusing too much on

what if

ground yourself in

what is

your emotional history
isn't just a set of memories

there are imprints in your subconscious,
habit patterns and blockages
caused by how you reacted
to what you felt in the past

healing is the unbinding and unloading
of your emotional history
through acceptance and letting go

sometimes we want to feel safer before moving forward by developing a clear plan, but this is not always possible. having a goal or an intuitive hunch is often enough to justify moving in a new direction.

even if a full plan is possible, you must not become too attached as you move through your journey. conditions change and unforeseen obstacles appear, requiring you to be flexible. during the journey a lot of learning can happen; taking in new experiences and data should inspire you to reassess your strategy so you can be more effective.

not knowing how everything will play out can feel daunting, but having a goal that drives you can function as a light through the dark unknown. if you take mindful steps that align with your values, intentionally treating yourself and others compassionately, then you will undoubtedly end up in a good place.

how long it takes matters much less than how much you learn and evolve as you move through the process.

real growth is refraining from making assumptions
so you can focus on observing

getting more information
so that you can develop a well-rounded view
is always better than letting yourself
be dominated by an impulsive reaction

tame your ego to let yourself see more

\

healing places you on a trajectory. first you focus on building self-awareness so that you can enhance your capacity to face your emotions, including those that are heavy and uncomfortable. this helps you see yourself more clearly as you move through your emotional spectrum and eventually understand how your emotions impact your actions.

once your clarity increases to the point that your major patterns are revealed, you start the serious work of building positive habits—new, more intentional responses to life that free you from the past.

as you learn to feel your emotions and better manage your reactions, the next empowering step is to bring harmony to your interactions, not by attempting to control others but by maintaining a balanced energy even when others invite you to join their turbulence. living in your peace will welcome others to choose peace as well.

aim to be a better person,
not a perfect person

don't fall into an attachment trap
where your expectations of yourself
are unreasonably high

find the balance between
raising the standard
and not punishing yourself
when mistakes or setbacks occur

emerging

there will be challenges

unwanted moments
unexpected heartache
unforeseen difficulties

times when you have no other option
but to face the chaos

life will ask you to stand tall and grow
even when you are tired

and in these moments of expansion,
you will see
that you are more than a match
for what scares you

you are stronger than you imagined

you know you have been away
from the present moment
for far too long

when your mind starts rehashing old grudges
and gets caught up in imaginary arguments

our society glorifies speed, big leaps forward, and meteoric rises, but reality usually moves at a slower pace, especially when it comes to personal transformation. not every day needs to involve a "big win" for you to end up in a thriving and beautiful place.

transformation isn't a smooth process. cloudy days are bound to happen. setbacks are natural. down moments are expected. often, it will feel like you are moving against a strong current of old conditioning. but with time and repetition, this resistance will soften, and the new you will come forward.

our task, as we develop new ways of living, is to embrace the idea that small, daily accomplishments are more valuable than fast results. this is how we build momentum for the long journey.

remember:

happiness is not achieved overnight,
peace takes time to build,
a healthy mind requires slow and gentle tending.

people who are willing to grow
emit an attractive vibe

even if you are just starting on your journey,
being comfortable with moving beyond old limits
gives off a special energy that calls in
other emotionally mature people

what can you do to connect with your true purpose and gifts?

when you start turning inward to heal and let go, you remove the layers of heavy conditioning and trauma that have been blocking your natural creativity from coming forward.

when your mind is lighter, it will more easily connect with its talents and genuine aspirations, and you will find a way to use those talents to serve others.

no one can show up 100% of the time

next time you feel upset for temporarily
not being the best version of yourself,
notice the attachment you have to perfection

remember that you occasionally need to slow down
and preserve your energy
to fully restore your well-being

a real conversation with a good friend
can be so powerfully healing

sometimes what you need
is to be truly vulnerable and feel completely seen

connecting with another person at such a deep level
can leave you feeling reenergized and refreshed

it is easier to step away from an argument
and remain calm

when you realize
they are not picking a fight with you;
they are actually fighting themselves

sometimes you just know
that the tension coming your way
is not about you at all

it is no surprise that you feel tired,
heavy, and short-tempered once you start
deeply engaging with your emotional history

healing will make you feel what you avoided,
and this may impact your mood

letting old burdens move through you is hard,
but it will help you feel renewed

with enough healing
there comes a point when
who you were before is truly gone

the old you literally becomes a thing of the past
more of a memory
than something with sway
or power over you

your identity feels less restricted by old pain
your perspective feels more expansive

reactive patterns have less control over you
and peace finally feels more accessible

this is a step toward freedom

on happiness

happiness is often confused with perfection; it is seen as a smoothness in external events where everything you like and love about life remains precisely abundant. the problem with perfection is that it is mythical; it is an imaginary pathway that, with enough time, will lead back to sorrow. being attached to perfection is not only a refusal to accept the ups and downs of reality but also a manifestation of the craving to control. life does not unfold in a straight and unbreakable line; its movements are choppy, unpredictable, more similar to waves in the ocean. and much of it is out of our control. giving external events a high degree of importance over how you feel inside will lead you far away from happiness.

happiness is also confused with the sensation of pleasure. whenever we come in contact with something agreeable, a subtle pleasant sensation will move through the body, and we react to it with craving. the problem with pleasure is that it quickly becomes an endless chase. we keep trying to place ourselves in situations that give us the feelings we are attached to. the unpopular truth is that the unbalanced pursuit of pleasure is a pathway that leads to dissatisfaction and sorrow. pleasure is so fleeting that it is not reliable enough to be the center of our lives.

solely seeking pleasure or perfection does not make for a fulfilling existence; it actually creates the conditions for superficial interactions, and it functions as a barrier that can stop you from getting to know every part of yourself. if your

continued

continued

attachment to pleasure is very high, then you will have a hard
time sitting with the hurt or traumatized parts of yourself.
being attached to perfection or pleasure can limit your ability
to be vulnerable with yourself and other people, because you'd
rather be immersed in something that is pleasant. anything
pleasant is incredibly temporary and will leave you with an
unquenchable thirst for more.

healing yourself is an opening to true happiness. letting go
of the mental burdens you carry from the past will help your
mind become clearer and more aligned with the natural flow
of life. often the hurt that weighs you down functions as a
wall that stops you from fully engaging with the present
moment. unprocessed hurt also limits the flow of compassion
because too much of our energy is focused on surviving one
day at a time. this hinders the ability to deepen interpersonal
connections. the happiness that is derived from being able to
exist peacefully in the present moment is a quality that must
be developed deliberately. happiness does not just happen; you
need to tend your inner garden, remove the weeds, and plant
the right seeds.

happiness is a product of equanimity, meaning mental balance
and the ability to be calmly objective. from this space of
clarity and composure, the real essence of happiness can
develop, which is inner peace. a type of peace that is not
controlled or defined by external events, one that can move
with the waves of life without getting overwhelmed

continued

or tossed around. happiness can multiply and enhance the
finer mental qualities that make life beautiful, like being able
to love yourself and other people or being able to see more
perspectives than just your own. at its core, happiness is
accepting reality and appreciating the miracle of the moment
without getting lost in the craving for more.

how do you build a good life?

relentlessly follow your intuition.
build with people who also love to grow.
take responsibility for your healing.
love yourself so deeply that you feel
at home in your own body and mind.
teach yourself to forgive.
never stop being a kind person.

saying less is incredibly helpful

not every thought is valuable
not every feeling needs to be voiced

what is often best is to slow down and spend time
developing a clearer and more informed
perspective

ego rushes and reacts,
but peace moves purposefully and gently

take a moment to be grateful
to your old self
for getting you this far

they kept going even when things got hard
and they said no to the temptation
of going back to old ways

their effort put you on a better path

by fully saying yes to growth,
they made your life today more fulfilling

if connection alone were enough,
there would be no breakups

connection needs the nourishment
of both partners cultivating
emotional maturity and self-awareness

when each of you embraces personal growth,
you can create a home spacious
and flexible enough to hold real love

maturity is when you don't need to hear
all the gossip or know a bunch of secrets

you support your inner peace by letting
the right information come to you instead of chasing
after the craving of knowing everyone's business

ego wants you to be at the center of everything,
but joy wants you to focus on your well-being

letting go is not always quick

often, it happens little by little

like when an old hurt comes up
and each time it has slightly less power over you

or when an old pattern reappears
and the struggle to say no to it
slowly becomes less intense

old layers take time to dissolve

there is a lot of freedom in not needing
to name all of your successes

not only does it keep you humble,
but it stops others from sending
jealous energy your way

quietly doing your best
helps good things flow
to you more abundantly

a big red flag is when
someone can't spend time alone

if they feel lost when no one is around
or when they are not in a relationship,
then they are deeply disconnected from themselves

the danger here is that they will use your presence
to avoid dealing with their own issues

this makes your time together unstable

you know you are developing wisdom
when you can strike an easier balance
between awareness of your own perspective
and consideration for the perspectives of others

you use your self-love to protect yourself
but you also have the humility
to know you are not always right

the ability to appreciate the perspective of another person is a great sign of personal growth. being able to see from different angles beyond the one that your lifelong conditioning has given you is possible only because you developed a healthy degree of letting go.

if your ego is too dominant, then your attachment to your own worldview becomes rigid. if your compassion has been amply cultivated through growth and healing, then your mind will have the flexibility it needs to set aside what it knows so that it can truly feel and listen to a perspective even if it is in contradiction to your own.

being able to consider the perspective of another does not negate your view. life is complex. multiple truths can exist alongside one another.

there is ignorance in holding only one perspective as supreme, because in every situation, there is more to know and see. being open to expansion is not only a pathway to happiness, it is an essential key that welcomes wisdom into your mind.

they asked her,

"how do you get through tough moments?"

she answered,

"do not trust the way you see yourself when your mind is turbulent, and remember that even pain is temporary. honor your boundaries, treat yourself gently, let go of perfection, and feel your emotions without letting them control you. you have enough experience to face the storm and evolve from it."

(resilience)

being willing to face your inner storms sometimes gets you so focused on your emotions and your past that you forget to look up and notice that you have taken many steps forward, that life is not the same anymore, and that your behaviors are more supportive of your happiness.

there is a moment of victory that eventually happens when you take your growth and healing seriously. you start to notice that you are no longer the same person who started the journey. every day is not a great day — there are still plenty of challenges — but there is a new freshness to life and the low points are not as low as they once were.

tough emotions don't control your actions the way they used to. when you do react, it is no longer as intense or overwhelming. you are not perfectly happy all the time, but that was never the goal. instead, you feel a new sense of calm because you've more deeply embraced the inevitability of change. you don't fear the ups and downs but have learned to glide with them.

joy is more available to you because you spend time cultivating your patience and your ability to appreciate the present moment. you know that there is still much to heal and more ways to grow, but you are familiar with the rhythm of observing, accepting, letting go, and allowing transformation to occur organically.

unpopular truth:

being around people who need nothing from you
can be deeply rejuvenating. it is hard to fill your
own tank when you are always around others
who need your help. make time for friends
who ignite your joy, fill you with laughter,
and recharge your inspiration.

an attachment to control
essentially comes from
having a bad relationship
with change

embracing change is one of the most understated ways to improve your life. a lot of the mental tension we experience comes from rejecting change. the common pattern is to lament that something pleasurable has ended or to roll in mental tension when something you dislike is occurring.

teaching your mind to ponder more about the reality of change will release some of the shock that comes when things actually do change in your life. understanding that change is inevitable will help you recognize that everything has a time limit, which ultimately encourages you to be more present when you are doing things that bring you joy or when you are around the ones you love.

too often we get caught up in our imagination, creating heavy narratives about the past or craving something in the future, altogether missing the beautiful moment that is right in front of us. every moment has potential, and that potential is defined by how we arrive into it. our minds have the power to turn a moment that might easily have been forgotten into something awe-inspiring and positively life-changing.

embracing change not only brings more joy into your life and enhances your resilience during tough moments but also is the key to happiness and wisdom. being attached to sameness dulls the vibrancy of life.

everyone who is healing their old trauma
and learning to live beyond the past
is part of the solution

happiness is not:

perfection, control, or determined
by external events and people.

happiness is:

a product of your perception and
inner balance. when you define your
own energy, you bring your harmony
with you wherever you go.

let yourself disappoint people,
especially if you need to take care of your mind
or because your intuition is telling you
that what they want does not align
with who you are becoming

betraying yourself is not virtuous

remember, no one can feel your heart
better than you can

being able to see yourself as you are moving through your
own emotional spectrum is an essential quality to cultivate.
knowing the difference between who you are when you are
balanced versus who you are when your mood is low can
help you endure difficult moments without making them
any harder.

when you are in a tense mood, question the assessments and
judgments you are making. you know from past experience
that heavy emotions negatively color your view. this is not the
time to make big decisions.

your perception is never perfect—it is influenced by your
emotions, or you may be missing some further information
that would clarify what you are seeing—understanding this
supports your humility.

perception becomes clearer when your mind is balanced and
when it tries to develop an assessment as selflessly as possible.
those with deep inner peace understand that there is rarely a
need to create a rigid judgment, that what are most needed are
love and care.

some people won't be able to see you,
even if you are standing right in front of them

they speak to you,
but they are only giving you their projections

they want you to listen,
and they think they know what's best for you,
even though they don't know you at all

what do you do when everything is going wrong?

don't punish yourself or think badly of yourself
remember that storms are temporary
try to do kind things for others
make changes to your daily routine
figure out which old habit is slowing you down
do what you need to do to balance your mind
and realign with your peace

you need your own definition of happiness

one that reconnects you with the beauty
of where you are now

and does not postpone your joy
until you accomplish something
in the future

one that is centered on embracing
and not striving

if you want to heal
and let go of the past,
you must deeply embrace
how you feel in the present

periodically, you will need to heal your motivations

it takes a significant amount of honesty with yourself
to realize that greed and fear have crept too far
into the center of your mind

needing to reconnect yourself
with your best intentions
does not mean you are moving backward;
it just means you are human

once you realize that the judgments of others are largely
informed by a combination of their old conditioning and
current emotion, it will give you the freedom to genuinely
be yourself.

the most common state of perception is an unclear one,
because our emotional history is evaluating everything we
encounter. people normally see you through the very thick
lens of their own past. letting your life be defined by the
judgments and assumptions others make of you is a quick path
to people-pleasing and constant dissatisfaction. if you want
to do your life justice, then you simply need to be kind, walk
gently, have compassion, and, above all, live in a way that
honors your truth.

it is possible to view others without judgment, to see them
through a lens of acceptance, but that takes intentional practice
and healing work to relieve yourself of the thickness of ego.
if ego is more dominant in your mind than compassion,
then it will be difficult to see beyond yourself. fortunately,
compassion is like any other muscle. as you train it, it will
become stronger. responding from a place of compassion
instead of ego is not only possible, it is essential to a
harmonious life.

if you embrace growth,
remain humble,
and are not afraid
of stepping outside of your comfort zone,
you can be sure that your best work
and the best parts of your life
have not happened yet

on control

if you were to take a deeper look at the foundation of nature,
you would see that at its creative core there is the swift flow
of movement. particles whizzing by at rapid speeds and
interacting in different combinations—temporary connections
breaking and forming. all that we know in daily life is
animated by the undercurrent of change. change creates the
space where mind and matter come together to construct the
illusion of self. it allows for endless possibilities and ensures
the deterioration of each new combination. nature exists in
the form of a river; to fight this never-ending flow is to cause
ourselves heartache and stress.

the ego seeks to control, so naturally it is at odds with the
truth of impermanence. the ego wishes to mold reality so that
it may have all that it craves, but that is not possible, nor is it
a path to happiness. the ego is bound together by attachment,
meaning the craving for things to exist in a certain way. the
ego struggles against change because change reveals that
control is rarely possible and at a deeper level that the ego
itself is ultimately insubstantial.

control has severe limits. the only parts of reality that we
have power over are our own actions and the habits that those
actions create. to think that we can manipulate all of reality
is a serious delusion, and if we are to act on that delusion
continuously, then it will become easy to harm those we come
across. control sucks the air out of relationships, and it pushes
away good people. control functions in opposition to love.

continued

long-lasting friendships and relationships often break under
the weight of control. the thicker the ego is, the more likely the
individual is to believe that their way is always the right way.
control is often a manifestation of old hurt and trauma.

at the apparent level of everyday life, you and i are here,
but at the ultimate level, we are simply temporary changing
phenomena. being able to live in balance with these two truths,
that we are real and that we are not real, actually helps us live
without holding on so intensely. when you deeply embrace
change, letting go becomes much easier. you can teach the ego
to exist more loosely by intentionally developing the qualities
of present-moment awareness and by challenging yourself to
selflessly witness the perspective of others. the highest levels
of happiness are not available unless you exist in harmony
with the truth of change, and that requires you to become more
flexible with your idea of who you are and what you desire.

it serves you best to flow with change, instead of fearing and
fighting it. you can simultaneously make decisions that align
yourself with your goals while also accepting that there will
be many moments in your life that you cannot control—all
you can really do is respond to the changes that occur in a way
that supports your freedom and happiness. relying on control
is an attempt at finding security, but that feeling of safety and
fullness will become abundant only when you can accept
change as your teacher. it is easier to stop having a combative
relationship with change when you remember that change

continued

continued

facilitates the creation of everything you love; without change
there is no existence. mold your life in the ways that you can,
especially when it comes to your own actions, but do not lean
on control as a way to heal or misconstrue it as a method for
joy. the deepest healing and delight arise from letting go.

you know you are moving in the right direction
when you think to yourself,

"i am so thankful to my recent past self
for making this current moment easier
than it would have been otherwise."

the work you put in now
makes your future brighter and smoother.

you don't need to rush your opinions
or make judgments on every topic

the agitation you feel to join the group
by quickly accepting the general outlook
limits your ability to be
the realest version of yourself

it's okay to move at your own pace
and to remain curious

together

i feel like i know you
but this is our first time meeting

my intuition tells me this is a new chapter
in our very old story

your eyes look familiar
and naturally i feel comfortable in your presence

i don't remember my past lives
but if i have lived previously
you were certainly there

if this is a new opportunity for us
let's make sure to do it all
better than before

don't look for perfect,
look for someone
who is ready to be real

don't look for beauty,
look for someone
who your intuition gravitates toward

don't look for no arguments,
look for someone
who is ready to discuss things with gentleness

emotional maturity does not create a flawless relationship;
it just prepares you to better handle the ups and downs
you're bound to experience while you learn to love each other
well. long conversations, tears, apologies, and embracing
vulnerability are common when the love is deep.

you can't build a relationship with someone
who wants everything their way

a red flag is when you keep trying to find a middle path
but you repeatedly end up with less than what is reasonable

someone who is insecure
and wants all the control
can't love you well

three undeniable green flags:

they understand that their emotional history
impacts how they show up in a relationship

they can embrace their emotions but
can also regulate their reactions

they do not expect that you will
be happy every single day

the reality of relationships
is that you are not going to be
the best versions of yourselves every day.

it is normal for there to be hard or slow days,
moments when your past comes up strongly,
and times where a lot of your energy
is simply focused inwardly on healing.

preventative communication can reduce unnecessary arguments. when you take the time to let your partner know where you are in your emotional spectrum (you feel down, sad, happy, short-tempered, etc.), it gives each of you the information you'll need to support each other well.

don't wait to be asked "how do you feel today?" volunteering the information, especially when you are in turmoil, can be so valuable to you both. it helps you admit to yourself what emotions are currently passing through you, and it gives your partner useful context for understanding your mood.

this level of communication can uplift self-awareness and cut down on projection. creating a culture of early communication within a relationship will not only invite greater vulnerability and depth; it will also help you to show each other loving support.

what you need one day may be quite different from the next. it is important not to expect your partner to read your mind. they simply can't do that. real love is about finding a middle path that you both feel good about.

healthy relationships will become more common
because people are letting go of their hurt
instead of projecting it onto everything they see

healing is based on compassionately
communicating with yourself;
this skill transforms the way
you approach your connections

fear and old hurt can make it hard to accept the selfless nature of love. in its highest forms, love is about giving, understanding, caring, and all qualities that arise when you can look at another in an egoless manner and act in their best interest.

some will ask: "if love is selfless, how do i go about taking care of myself?"

the answer is that the love between two people must be in balance with each partner's self-love. from self-love arises the communication of needs and the active commitments that help both feel nourished.

yes, love is about giving, but self-love is about doing what you must to enhance your inner light. it is about knowing your own limits. treating yourself well is critical if you want to build harmony with another human being.

the interaction between love for another and self-love should help form a balance where both people can aspire to be selfless but at the same time are clear on what they need so that their personal thriving can be supported.

11 relationship goals:

act as a team
no manipulation
honest communication
handle conflict peacefully
make time to relax together
share decision-making power
create space for vulnerability
find joy in each other's happiness
be open about your fears and goals
let your healing deepen your connection
try to understand each other's perspective

elements of a healthy relationship

personal transformation that is grounded in self-love and has greater inner peace as its goal will naturally teach you to love others well. on the journey to improve your own mental state, you will improve your ability to connect. relationships are unique, but there are a few outstanding qualities that help them be healthy.

embracing growth: when both individuals have the courage and humility to see themselves as imperfect human beings who still have much to learn, there is a greater opportunity for harmony to enter the relationship. harmony is possible when each person can own their mistakes and seek to correct them. understand that friction is still bound to arise, but both partners can combat needless conflict by building self-awareness and resisting ego-driven narratives.

listening selflessly: it is important to develop both patience and presence in a relationship. without these qualities, it is impossible to listen to your partner in an egoless manner. both people have their own version of what is happening, and each individual deserves to be listened to. when two people can actively take turns listening to each other selflessly, with the sole goal of taking in one another's perspective, it helps them build the understanding that is needed for harmony to arise.

understanding over winning: normally, we seek to win arguments, but that framing creates a situation in which one person is bound to lose. relationships should never be about

continued

continued

domination. it is much healthier to approach conflict with a goal of understanding. when you understand one another and can meet each other in the middle, there won't be much left to argue about, and it becomes easier to let go of the conflict entirely. when understanding is the goal, arguments tend to be shorter and lighter. they can even foster a deeper connection.

supporting each other's power: taking turns being the leader in different situations helps each individual express their power and talents. partners normally have different strengths, so it makes sense that one person is not always in control of every moment. sharing power is critical to creating a harmonious environment in which trust can flourish. being able to live in your power creates the sense of freedom that we all need to truly feel at home.

it's natural for relationships
to include moments of monotony and simplicity

similar to spending time alone,
both of you peacefully accepting slow moments
means you have healthy connections with yourselves

appreciating the mundane aspects of life
as a couple is a sign that you have
both grown so much

deep relationships will periodically need
intentional rebalancing
so that both people feel supported
in their power and happiness

what worked before
may not work well now
because you have both grown so much

be honest about what you need
so you can create a more nourishing union

how do you get over a breakup?

let yourself accept what has happened. it is natural to feel
sadness. what makes breakups harder than they need to be is
our tendency to get stuck in imagining the past and craving
what is no longer there. the only way forward is to keep
bringing yourself back to the present moment.

there is no set timeline or path to healing because each heart
is unique. what you can do is work on your self-love: give
yourself what you have been seeking from others; feed your
needs; connect with good friends and find joy in the small
moments of life. self-love is especially important because it
is a gateway to letting go of the past.

this is a good time to build new habits that align you with a
more fulfilling life. it can also be helpful to reassess what you
are actually looking for in a partner. more than anything, your
own self-acceptance will make you feel whole. let this be a
period of healing and evolution that radically improves
your life.

the freedom you feel when you realize that
you don't need their apology to move forward

you just need your own self-love
and acceptance to let it go

now you can let your intuition and higher standards
lead you to connecting with people who are
emotionally available and aligned

instead of saying "i am sad"

reframe it to

"sadness has temporarily appeared"

or "sadness is passing through me"

maturity in a relationship is
when you can both be calmly grumpy
at the same time
without taking it out on each other

sometimes moods become heavy
without a substantial cause

refusing to give your temporary feeling
an unjustified narrative
or any control
is a powerful way to love someone well

ask yourself:

in what areas of your life do you find yourself clinging to control?

how would being more open to change affect your relationships?

is there an unchangeable situation that you are working on accepting?

what can you currently do to love yourself better?

in what ways have you been living intentionally recently?

you are not helping well
if you are doing so to the point
of exhaustion and burnout

love doesn't mean giving
until you have nothing left

if you are taking it this far,
that's a sign that self-love is lacking

tend to your own needs
and return to balance

find a partner who does not expect you to be constantly happy or high energy because they have enough emotional maturity to embrace ups and downs. relationships do not exist in an eternal spring; they go through seasons in a way that propels your personal growth. real love understands that moods fluctuate, especially when healing is helping you take steps forward. you both use communication during down moments to let each other know that heaviness is passing through your mind and to figure out the best ways to support each other. you have both decided to take the route of authenticity because that is the fastest way for you to truly shine your brightest and for you to deepen your connection.

relationships built on beauty and lust do not have the
foundation for a long-lasting union. much more than this is
needed to build an enduring partnership. it is more substantial
to fall in love with who a person is, their mannerisms, their
resilience and brilliance, the way they move about the world,
the decisions they make, their aspirations and values, and most
importantly the way their being feels naturally right sitting
next to yours. these qualities are not normally apparent on the
surface. it takes wanting to know someone on a deeper level
to fully appreciate how special they are.

you may fall in love with someone for who they are in that
moment, but mature relationships leave space for each
person to grow and evolve. the person you fall in love with
initially will not remain the same throughout the entirety
of your relationship. if the connection is strong and if your
commitments have created a safe and rejuvenating home, then
it won't be difficult to fall in love with each other again and
again. part of loving a partner well is getting to know the new
aspects of their personality as they emerge. loving each other
for who you are now, instead of who you were then, keeps the
relationship fresh and focused on the present.

they asked her,

"what qualities should your partner have?"

she answered,

"above all, the willingness to grow and enough
self-awareness so they can truly love you well. if
they are emotionally prepared for a real connection
and ready for the deep healing that will bring you
closer together over time, it will be easier to build
a nourishing and vibrant home. real love is a
commitment to supporting each other's happiness."

(conscious love)

relationships are not about constantly catering to each other; they are about growing together through the ups and downs. of course, supporting each other's happiness is important, but relationships are not a never-ending blissful paradise. nothing in life is perfectly pleasant all of the time.

detaching from the idea that every day should be high energy and joyful makes room for a deeper level of love. a relationship is meant to be a journey, one on which you are bound to come across the unhealed parts of yourself. a truly loving union is a truth-telling mirror. you will see the rough parts of your ego and many of the areas where growing will help you become a happier individual and a better partner.

love is the internal discovery of self-awareness and selflessness; it is the overcoming of ego and the healing of old wounds so you can turn outward and show up for yourself and others in a much more nurturing way.

the deepest and most healing friendships
are often shared between people who are
very different from one another

what keeps the bond strong
is each friend's embrace of personal growth

as they evolve and transform,
the love and care endure,
because they do not fear change

you need to know when to walk away

if misalignment feels constant and harmony is rare

if their words are unreliable
and the support you need to flourish
is clearly not within their emotional capacity

no longer feeding a connection
that is losing its energy is a hard choice,
but it might be the exact thing
you need to do
to honor your self-love
and personal growth

you know you have made serious progress
when you encounter someone's rough emotions
and instead of letting their volatility consume you,
you mentally affirm within yourself
"i will not join them in their turbulence."

find a partner who increases your power
instead of diminishing it. complementing
each other's qualities in a way that helps both of you
shine brighter is an immense gift.
you not only lend your strengths to each other,
you also feed the spark that inspires evolution.

the quickest way to squander a beautiful connection is
attachment, meaning the craving to have things occur in
a very particular way. often, attachment is exacerbated by
fears that stem from our unhealed emotional history.

tumultuous and unobserved emotions snowball into
insecurities that strengthen the misguided idea that pursuing
our attachments is the only way to create safety and abundance
in our lives. our hurt tricks us into thinking that the only way
to keep love is to cling to it. insecurity will manifest itself as
control, which blocks the flow of real love.

the truth is that only open hands can carry love well; hands
that are closed tightly cannot receive or give love. love's
closest synonym is freedom, which means that love is not
something that can thrive in a constricted environment. love
needs space to stretch, expand, and flow.

a common fear is that without the constraints of attachments
and expectations, love will never last. love between two
people does require a middle ground where both can meet,
but attachments cannot provide this space because they are
far too rigid.

healthy love creates its middle ground through calm
communication and voluntary commitments. commitments
are mutually agreed-upon actions and ways of being that
both partners feel good about. they work because they are
simultaneously sturdy and flexible. when two partners decide
that their needs or wants have shifted, they can also shift how

continued

continued

they show up for each other in the relationship. harmonious partners align their commitments with their growth and with support for each other's happiness.

find a partner who realizes how their emotional history impacts the way they show up in your relationship. they don't need to know themselves perfectly or have healed all their old hurt; they just need enough self-awareness to see when their past is getting in the way of loving you well. they know that rough emotions from the past have a way of twisting the mind so that it stirs up unnecessary arguments. together, you lean on honesty with yourselves and each other to help get you through difficult moments. you support each other whenever old pain needs attention. you wholeheartedly agree that loving each other deeply and healing yourselves should be your top priority.

connections often break under the weight
of unresolved trauma and poor communication

old hurt creates distance between partners
and makes it hard to see each other clearly

without selfless listening
and vocalizing your vulnerability,
it will be difficult to deepen your bond

if they are constantly projecting,
blaming others for their own emotions,
and not interested in personal growth,

then it will be tough to build a healthy
relationship together.

connection is not enough.

partnerships also require a certain amount
of emotional preparedness.

when you can't deal with your pain,
you suppress it or project it

the hurt you carry darkens
what you see

falling in love with the wrong person
and choosing not to love the right person
are common situations
that are not talked about enough

cravings, old hurt, and dense conditioning
can confuse the heart

sometimes it takes years to fully realize that

what you see on social media
can give you unrealistic expectations
of what a healthy relationship should be

you're not going to be your best every day
you will sometimes say the wrong thing
communication isn't always clear
you won't always agree

things don't have to be "perfect"
for the relationship to be profoundly fulfilling

love can be tough to navigate
when the mind is constantly
craving more

craving often blocks us from seeing
the incredible person standing
right in front of us

craving also disconnects us from gratitude

emotional maturity is not:

handling everything on your own
or being beyond your emotions

emotional maturity is:

feeling tough emotions without
feeding them or projecting
your tension onto others

find a partner who can match your emotional capacity. if they can feel the depth of their personal ups and downs without running away, they will be able to show up in your relationship during moments of both victory and struggle. when partners know how to meet their own emotions with presence, there will be more harmonious understanding between them and less knotted-up confusion. the way each partner meets themselves as an individual is reflected in the compassion and patience they offer each other. neither partner has to be perfect or have it all figured out. what makes it all work is that the love between you is not alone; it is enhanced by your commitments to grow, let go, heal, and unbind what no longer serves.

strong relationships are not about
getting it right every single time

they are about embracing the fact
that each person has a lot of growing to do
and loving each other through the process

you both handle conflict by trying to
understand each other
instead of being combative

the connection brings you together,
but the emotional maturity is what makes it work

it is not about finding a partner who is fully healed;
it is about finding someone who is not afraid of their emotions.
a person who does not suppress what they feel
and can gently be present with their inner ups and downs
will have a foundation of emotional maturity.

one of the most important skills to develop
in a relationship is knowing when to step back
and give your partner space when they are
having a tough time or when to step up
and give active support. the type of love
they could use to help them through their
process will not always be the same.

give support, but don't try to fix everything
embrace growth, but don't expect perfection
have boundaries, but change them as needed
have determination, but rest and relax as well
allow connection, but build with mature people
be positive, but let yourself feel hard moments

direction

11 personal commitments:

live with gratitude
believe in your power
self-love is not optional
heal at your own speed
don't glorify being busy
don't rush important things
stop doubting your progress
only commit to what feels right
use boundaries to help you focus
listen when your intuition says yes
put your energy into your highest goals

bring your own vibe to the situation.
let your inner light shine even if it shakes up the room.
no more conforming.
no more waiting for another day to be you.

lean into your personal energy
by connecting with your real goals.

make the moves that will brighten your future.

it is possible to live with kindness and compassion toward yourself and others while also creating healthy boundaries or defending yourself when it is actually necessary. you can be gentle with the world and also protect your own flourishing. instead of resorting to survival mode when life gets hard, reclaim your power by taking your time to respond skillfully.

some friends deserve a whole chapter
in the story of your life. things wouldn't
be as good had they not been around
to support you through unbearable storms
and tell you those few hard truths that
encouraged your evolution. their essential
light helped you discover your own.

if you really want to rebel in a
narrow-minded and egocentric society,
be more loving.
care more widely and vocally.
boldly live from your heart.
give without fear.
find joy in being selfless.
share your talents.
live without needing permission.

when your self-love increases,
you become far less willing to harm others

why?

because real self-love slowly opens
the door to unconditional love for all beings

4 life lessons:

build inner peace or fall to outer chaos

being flexible does not mean giving up

appreciate the closest friends in your life

challenging times do not last forever

the few solid friends you can be super real with,
who legitimately have your back, outweigh in
value the multitude of other connections you have
that aren't as deep. many friendships promise a lot
but don't actually amount to much in the end.
the friends who truly make time for you are
worth more than a thousand acquaintances.

they asked her,

"how do you know the healing is working?"

she answered,

"when your mind is no longer governed by the
past and when you feel peace in situations where
you used to feel tension. you more easily connect
with joy and happily use boundaries to protect your
well-being. the healing is real when your mind feels
lighter and loving yourself comes more naturally."

(progress)

what do you do when everything is going right?

embrace the moment without letting it get to your ego
find more ways to help others
balance your mind by remembering that nothing lasts forever
keep making the same good decisions that got you here
enjoy without getting attached

down moments will try to make you forget
how much you have actually accomplished

you have overcome too much to let heavy
emotions confuse you

stop listening to the noise
and ground yourself in the fact
that storms do not last forever

trauma reacts; intention responds

the intensity of your reaction reveals
how much of the past you are holding on to

forgiveness is powerful medicine. hate weighs heavily on the mind.

feeling intense aversion to someone is a sign of attachment because there is something there that we refuse to move past or let go of. not only does this keep our energy pointed in the direction of the past, it keeps the mind rolling in turbulence.

you may feel aversion to someone because of something they did to you, but feeling that same intensity toward them repeatedly, long after the incident has passed, does more damage to you than to them. if the simple thought of them makes your mind react with heaviness and repugnance, that means you are giving them too much of your mental space.

when you take your evolution into your own hands, you do the work of reclaiming your power—in this case this means returning your energy back to you by not letting your reactions drag you back to what happened in the past.

seek a middle ground where you let go and simultaneously let the past inform you instead of control you. total forgiveness is freedom. even if you struggle to fully pardon them in your heart, you can still make some peace with the past so you can finally experience peace in your mind.

one of the best ways to love your partner well
is by simply not projecting your tough emotions onto them

tell your partner when you feel internally rough
and pay attention to the way temporary emotions
impact the narratives in your mind

this will stop so many arguments from happening

throw away the idea
that letting go is quick
and is needed only once

the bigger the hurt,
the deeper it is carved into the mind

unbinding old patterns
and building healthy responses to life
are long-term projects

healing requires patience and repetition

be intentional and do not give up

it is easy to point fingers,
but when you look deeply within,
you see that you actually have a say
over how you react,
even during tough moments

you need to know who you are
or you'll be told who you are

loved ones and society can inundate you
with opinions and information

knowing your values can help you navigate the world

find the balance between embracing new ideas
and not being told what to think by others

feeling emotionally exhausted
is common after opening up deeply
or after experiencing a series of heightened emotions
for an extended period of time.

be prepared to take the quiet time
and solitude you need to fully rejuvenate.
you are allowed to not be serious all of the time.

find a partner who loves the real you and does not ask you to
conform to an image of perfection they carry in their mind.
when both of you release the attachment to perfection, your
love deepens, your connection grows stronger, and new space
opens for joy to flourish. you support each other in growing,
but you don't make demands or set silent expectations.
instead, you focus on creating an environment of security,
acceptance, and nourishment, so that each of you feels safe
to go inward and heal the old pain that limits you. a love that
lasts is a love that welcomes vulnerability and imperfection.

they asked her,

"how do you love yourself well?"

she answered,

"make your well-being and healing a top priority.
have the courage to create boundaries that will
support your flourishing. listen closely to your intuition,
respect your need for rest, and connect with people
who are emotionally available. being intentional
with your life is loving yourself well."

(conscious living)

double down on love

not the superficial love that ignores reality or history,
but the real love that is ready to move mountains

the type of love that is not afraid of action,
change, or personal growth

the type of love
that wants the best for all people,
including yourself

your ego
wants other people
to think
and act just like you

when you meet yourself again
after a long period of healing and growth,
you may feel clumsy with your words and actions
as you learn more about the new you

rebirth is not easy,
but now you have the mental agility
to go inward
and fully connect with your authenticity

when you commit to growth, your old habits will not make
it easy. often, doubt will roar and shout and try to trick you
into thinking you've made much less progress than you
really have. the mind likes to retrace its deepest grooves
again and again, weaving a dense barrier to change. luckily,
with persistence, you can work through even the densest
mental patterns, establishing new pathways that nourish you.
persistence is your greatest asset in your transformational quest.

it is not always time to grow

find the balance between
staying committed to your evolution
and taking time off from continuously
advancing to new levels

being where you are with intention
and enjoying how far you have come
help break the attachment to always craving results

making time for integration
makes lifelong growth
more sustainable

there are people who enjoy misunderstanding things

they will not attempt to take a genuine look
because they get too much pleasure from disliking
or their ego is too invested in twisting what they see

if you can't reason with them,
focus on preserving your energy
and go on living your life

11 ways to support your evolution:

read more
meditate daily
say no more often
be a clear communicator
decrease your screen time
let your top goals take priority
connect with people who inspire you
be kind but don't be a people pleaser
remember that rest supports creativity
don't let your past control your present
let go of competition so you can be yourself

create what your intuition is asking you to create. do this as an act of service. you have no idea whom you may end up helping or even the lives you may save simply by following the truth of your heart.

don't let fear stop you from listening to your inner calling. don't let an unclear path discourage you from taking steps into the unknown. the greatest you arises when you begin to embrace the space beyond your comfort zone.

you don't need to have all the answers right now to eventually be successful. you just need to be willing to take one step at a time. embrace the challenge. remember how strong you are and how much you have already overcome.

you don't need to move quickly. even slow movement will get you where you want to go. let yourself live in your power. you hold a unique vision, and that is your gift to the world.

jealousy is a clear sign
that you need to accept and love yourself more

being inspired by someone is totally different,
the energy is uplifting and brings the mind clarity
instead of heaviness

inspiration takes you further and helps you focus;
jealousy is the ego's insecurity

if you need to take it slow,
do so boldly

the speed of society can be exhausting

technology can feel draining

the false sense of competition
that exists in your mind
can decrease your happiness

personal success is more likely
when you focus on your path
and live without rushing

you have made immense progress

your self-awareness has reached new levels

your healing has made your mind less reactive

and you are now emotionally prepared for deeper connections

storms and challenges came but you are still standing strong

keep doing what is right for you

i thought we would have more time

the end was not just unwanted;
it was completely unexpected

when trouble arose,
i hoped things would quickly return to normal

i was not ready to have a new chapter forced upon me
and to be handed such a heavy feeling of loss

i must learn to tend to my heart in new ways
because you are no longer there to help me hold it

all i have in front of me
is the great task of creating
a new idea of happiness and home

it was not time that healed you;
it was your courage to feel everything
you used to run from

being with yourself and meeting your tension
is hard, but it is the only way to release what
has been bottled up inside of you

your pain was simply asking for your attention

let there be space between you
and what you believe in

attachment to what you think you know
can harden you and stunt your growth

there are certainly things we can know,
but knowledge is always incomplete
in a universe that is ever-changing

ego does not enjoy evolution,
it prefers sameness and control

the wisest among us say that ultimate freedom
results from the release of all ideas, all knowing,
only then can we transcend and observe what is

confidence

wisdom is not loud
nor does it whisper

it is a resonance
that realigns you with a better direction
it is a knowing that arises with undeniable clarity
it is an expansion that makes the mind lighter

wisdom is gradual,
often showing you the same truth
but from different angles,
until finally it clicks so deeply
that it becomes part of your being

as the wisdom within you matures,
it becomes easier to let go,
to stop fighting yourself,
and to move with nature instead of against it

instead of forcing yourself to let go

be still
be present
let yourself feel
don't run away
accept what is
and let it all unravel naturally

the battle is over
i'm done fighting myself

stressing over what i've done
or what i should have done
simply does not help

i want to see myself without pointing fingers
to move forward with grace
to see mistakes as lessons
and allow them to improve
my future actions

instead of being attached to the past
i want to peacefully connect to the present

healing happens
in the present moment

remember that
when you are focusing
way too much on the past

if you want to elevate your life
to the higher vision your intuition
tells you is possible,
you must be ready to accept
that those close to you may not believe in you at first

stepping away from what's common
by doing something totally unexpected
strikes fear in many

realize how short the walk is from gratitude to happiness

boundaries are the most direct way for you to protect
your energy.

make them clear for your sake. if they aren't, people will
just keep taking more and more, not maliciously, but because
they won't know when you need space or when you are
feeling depleted.

creating boundaries is a proactive way of designing your life.
to help maintain your inner and outer vibrancy, you must
decide with clarity who and what can enter your space and
when. boundaries are not about being overly strict or mean;
they are about using your awareness of what is genuinely good
for you to build a sanctuary that supports your growth.

in a world where there is a constant battle for your attention
and a potentially overwhelming amount of information, you
need proper digital and in-person boundaries to support your
mental health.

the memory of the past
can sometimes fade quickly

but the way you reacted
to what you felt in the past
can stay with you for years

it is easier to forget details
than to remove
the emotional imprints you carry

real healing isn't about forgetting;
letting go requires deep introspection
and acceptance

the way you impulsively react shows how you coped
or defended yourself in the past

if you are stuck in a defensive mode,
your mind will view things through
the fearful lens of survival

the key to arriving in the present
and breaking with the past
is to slow down

breathe
think
act

you are not always going to get it right. sometimes the reaction will be too strong, and it will pull you into saying and doing things that are counterproductive. if the trigger is too intense or if you are already in a low mood or exhausted, your reactions can more easily govern your thoughts and behavior.

even if you have grown immensely, you are not flawless. this is why growth is nonlinear. healing is not about developing an attachment to perfection; it is about recognizing the moments when you're moving in the opposite direction from your long-term goals and building awareness around what you can do differently next time.

recognizing when you get it wrong is not an invitation to be hard on yourself. in fact, it is a sign of victory. it means you can see yourself better than you did in the past, and you understand what areas you need to grow in next. real self-love embraces personal growth, but it does so gently.

the work you put into
a relationship that has ended
is not wasted

learning to love better,
to communicate clearly,
having the courage to speak up
about what you need,
and knowing how to give
without exhausting yourself

these are skills that will benefit
every part of your life

i am less interested in debating
and more interested in
considering a topic collectively

let's peacefully share
what we know with each other

when we arrive at diverging points of view,
let's focus on questions

how did you arrive at this point?

can you help me understand what you mean?

the default is to live from a place of ego,
focused on surviving

the goal is to live from a place of compassion
for yourself and others,
which supports thriving

some of my favorite people
are the ones who don't let society rush them.

they move at speeds that feel
more natural to their being.

they have their own idea of success
that is based on inner thriving,
and they treat their minds with gentle care.

above all, they embrace growth
the same way they embrace air and water,
because they see life as a gift that encourages
evolution.

different people and environments
bring out different sides of you,
not because you are fake or performative
but because your personality is expansive

who you are is an enormous spectrum;
let yourself flow so your identity can
express itself fully

you are not one thing;
you are unlimited

focusing on a few fundamentals can create a massive change
in your life:

1. make your healing, personal transformation,
   and well-being top priorities

2. refrain from harming yourself or others

3. create mental space for gratitude

4. be kind and generous to others

shifting your focus to growth and inner evolution will not
only decrease the tension in your mind but also automatically
change the way you relate to the ups and downs of life. the
law of cause and effect is pervasive through this universe of
mind and matter. being generous in a balanced way does bring
good results, but there is no telling when the fruit of your good
actions will ripen. if you are dedicated to cultivating inner
peace, it is essential to understand that the kindness you give
to others will fundamentally support your inner clarity
and calm.

beware of taking things to an extreme. many of us have the tendency to push ideas to the point where they make us act in an unbalanced manner and narrow our thinking. allow room in your mind for nuanced views and different perspectives. understand that the solutions that worked in one area may not work in another. life is very situational, meaning every circumstance will have a different set of conditions that calls for unique approaches. one size does not fit all. your middle path will not look like someone else's middle path. a good idea will remain good only if it is applied in a balanced way. balance is one of the keys to living a good life.

stop thinking better things come only
when you act flawlessly

get rid of strict time limits
for accomplishing your goals

say no when negativity tries to take your power

the ones who succeed are those who accept
that the journey is long and who keep going
even when things get hard

an eon's worth of sorrow
pain gathered through the ages
an ancient feeling of loss

the struggle has continued
inside of you
for long enough

the light of acceptance
settles the agitation
and opens the door to letting go

what you felt before
will not always leave quietly

sometimes the past will roar
through your sensations
as you cut the root
of what you held for far too long

(silence)

7 timeless values:

compassion
self-love
curiosity
balance
humility
growth
kindness

healing is a deconditioning process that ignites personal transformation. to let go is to literally release old parts of ourselves. a difficulty many of us come across on our inner journey is being able to release our attachment to who we used to be. how we see the world, our preferences, our likes and dislikes, and much more will shift and morph as we align with the genuine expression of our inner evolution.

we may at times feel odd when we outgrow the preferences we were familiar with. we may even feel a little lost when we realize that we have outgrown our old life. in these moments, it helps to remind ourselves that it is fine to have new favorites, new ways of expressing ourselves, new friends, and new aspirations. to fully embrace growth, we must be willing to venture into the unknown.

9 essentials for mature relationships:

share leadership
communicate often
tell each other the truth
do personal healing work
support each other's happiness
listen to each other's perspective
tell each other when you feel down
have your own interests and friends
make clear commitments to each other

they asked her,

"can time heal you?"

she answered,

"you are the key to your healing, not time. hurt, trauma, and
dense conditioning will continue sitting in your mind, impacting
your emotions and behavior, until you go inward. what heals is
self-love, learning to let go, self-awareness, and building
new habits."

(intention)

the future you needs your determination

say yes to the hard things that make you better

diligently build the habits that set you free

unapologetically create a life of your own design

every moment of effort enhances your vibrancy
and sets you up for a majestic existence

the best days of your life
can't happen without you there

live with presence

live intentionally

it's the friends who help you reconnect
with your original mission and values
who make a substantial difference in your life

sometimes it just takes one conversation
with someone who is radically authentic
to reignite your inner fire
and help you get back on the right path

your relationship with change
will define your life

if you reject change,
you will struggle

if you accept it,
it will inspire you
to be more present
and to live without holding back

find a partner who not only wants to love you right but also is
emotionally prepared to create a home. your natural attraction
is just the beginning; you both know that the health of your
relationship is directly linked to your personal growth and
the healing of reactive patterns. internally, you both feel
ready to share the work of love and to build a culture of calm
communication. the way you laugh as one and handle storms
with gentleness helps you cultivate a nurturing environment.
you understand that each of you has your own identity
that moves like a river—always changing, expanding, and
evolving—but the beauty of your love rests on your choice
to flow together, side by side.

ego is at work whenever you are looking down on someone, judging them harshly, and writing them off as permanently toxic or too far gone to redeem themselves. ego is incredibly sneaky; you can do a lot of inner work and get yourself to a better place and still have moments when ego twists your logic and clouds what you see.

the overuse of the words "toxic" and "narcissist" shows not only that there is a lack of compassion in how we deal with each other but also that it is becoming trendy to expect others not to make any mistakes.

there are obviously people out there who have caused harm, but we must make sure that we find a healthy middle path where we create safe spaces for ourselves without expecting perfection from everyone we encounter.

you know from your own experience how easy it is to make a mistake or to be totally misunderstood by another individual. perception is often untrustworthy, stunningly unclear, and dependent on personal emotional history.

the challenge is to elevate your personal transformation to a point where you can use boundaries to create space for yourself to thrive, without letting your ego use the dislike of people or things to inflate itself.

letting go will ask more of you:

more honesty
more self-awareness
more embracing change
more time healing old hurt
more time nurturing yourself
more listening to your intuition
more acceptance of all emotions
more present-moment awareness
more reprogramming of the subconscious

not everyone will understand
that you've changed

that the healing was necessary and real

some may keep seeing you as who you were before

but that's okay

they can't define you

your transformation taught you
not to let your spirit be diminished
by other people

your healing creates waves that are consciously and unconsciously felt by others. the vibration or energy you emit moves outward and influences your environment and those in it. your peace can be felt by others and invites them to remain in tune with the peace they already carry within themselves.

your sense of balance during difficult times is not only a pillar others can lean on, it shows them that they, too, can remain calm during a storm. sometimes people may even say to you, "it feels great and calming to be around you."

what we feel within us functions like an invitation for others to join us and feel the same, whether it is dense and heavy emotions or light and caring ones. when someone close to you gets angry, it's easy to match that anger with your own because the wounds of the past remain deep within your subconscious and are easily activated and pulled to the surface.

a powerful sign of maturity is the ability to dwell in the mind-state of your choice, even when others fill your shared space with negativity. being able to live within the energy of your choosing is a sign of great emotional development.

when you choose peace, it supports the peace in others.

no more lowering basic standards
and no tolerating mistreatment

give your time to people who
are revitalizing and emotionally
prepared for deep connection

3 ways to keep your energy strong as you move forward:

1. support your peace by not becoming extremely busy. give your time to what matters most and repeatedly let go of the rest.

2. feel good about saying no often so you can focus on what you truly want to pursue. if it does not click with your intuition, it is not for you.

3. don't let the emotional turbulence in others stop you from keeping your mood the way you want it to be.

wisdom has a timeless quality. throughout history, when people have sought wisdom, similar truths have appeared again and again. these are the lessons we must learn if we are to know true freedom. you cannot know peace without the full embrace of change. you cannot feel the deepest love without letting go of ego. you cannot fully enjoy the wellspring of happiness without trying to understand the depths of suffering.

distraction is part of the journey
it is surprisingly easy to lose your way
to take a detour
that eats up too much of your time
to lose sight
of the initial goals that animated your spirit

glamour can be compelling
busyness can cloud your vision
too much pleasure can leave you dull

and all the while a quiet agitation
begins to build

the uneasiness you feel when you
turn away from your goals

but because you have spoken your purpose
within the walls of your heart
you will not be able to stray too far
from your greatest aspiration

the higher path
will start calling you back
the light that was beginning to dim
will roar again

when you begin to see yourself clearly
your choices will realign with what is best
and you will rediscover your true way forward

you know the healing is real when you find more joy in unexpected places. when the wind touches your face gently and you cannot help but smile. when you look into the eyes of a friend and know that the connection you share has become deeper. when you feel the strength of having overcome so much and the lightness of no longer carrying as many past burdens. life itself has a radiant shimmer that you can more easily tap into. not only are you tuned into the boundless joy of the universe, you can easily flow with a path that leads you to greater inner and outer success.

humans are built for redemption
we are born into imperfection
and live it daily

but just as we can make mistakes,
we can also learn

with enough conviction,
we can understand where we went wrong,
break from the past,
and learn better
and kinder ways
of existing

on change and freedom

the power of impermanence is vastly underrated and easy
to overlook. we understand at the intellectual level that
everything is fundamentally governed by the law of change,
but when life throws its challenges or when we come upon a
moment in our lives that we deeply crave to last, the truth of
change falls into the shadows of forgetfulness. change is so
predominant in the structure of reality that being absentminded
of it will inevitably result in dissatisfaction, stress, and even
suffering.

the greatest adversary of the ego is change because the ego
arises out of the craving to survive, which means it will
attempt to control and keep things the same. since reality is a
moving river, our inner and outer flourishing is dependent on
our profound embrace of change. if ego is akin to survival,
then the acceptance of change is akin to freedom.

the ego craves a static existence because it thinks that this
is the only path to security, but the greatest security we can
cultivate is the release of attachments that comes from our
acceptance of change. a mind that is less attached can love
more powerfully and completely than one that is bogged down
with the denseness of craving to keep things the same. the
deeper you travel down the path of embracing change, the
easier it becomes to unleash love for yourself and all beings.

understanding that the tight attachment of the ego exists in
contradiction to the flowing and open movement of reality

continued

continued

is actually an invitation to cultivate the present-moment
awareness that allows us to live in harmony with nature.
it is only in the present moment when we can elevate our
intellectual understanding of change into the evermore
rewarding firsthand experience of change.

the acceptance of change not only opens the door to inner
peace but also welcomes you into the deeper insights that
ultimately lead to liberation. to be liberated, from the stress
and tension that come with attachment, is a challenging and
long path but one that is worth walking. as you take steps
along the path, the truth of change will not only elevate
your ability to love but also make it easier to deepen your
connection with yourself and others. change will implore you
to develop a dynamic identity, one where you allow yourself
to let go of old parts of you so you can evolve.

at even higher levels, change will expose the insubstantial
quality of the ego by revealing that all that is within you is
movement itself. as the rigidity of the ego diminishes, more
space is created for love and goodwill. some may wonder,
what happens if there is no ego; how will we live? our
mental framework would be structured around compassion
for ourselves and others; our motivations will emerge from a
balanced selflessness. at the level of everyday life, you will
function as a more expansive and selfless version of you.

peace is not:

having a life with no problems or having
everything happen the way you want it to

peace is:

having the wisdom to handle change without
stress; it is having a balanced mind
amid the ups and downs of life

as time moves forward, the world will continue changing
in small and large ways. this earthly realm moves between
calmness and storms. if the greater world is so unsteady and
uncontrollable, how do you move forward?

the only real option is to move in alignment with virtues that
support your inner peace: living your truth, remaining honest,
treating those you encounter with gentleness and respect,
being generous, and saying yes only to what is realistic for
you.

above all, stay in communion with your intuition. let it guide
you even when the path forward is unclear. walking this
earth gently, without the intention to harm others, will attract
kindness in return.

don't expect that others will always return the kindness you
show them. sometimes they will, but the kindness you give
may also return to you from new and unexpected people. do
not give to get. give so that others may live more vibrantly.

let your noble actions create a peaceful path for you to walk
on. there will undoubtedly be times when things get hard.
in those moments, do not stray from the qualities that have
helped you live a good life. jealousy, anger, hatred, and spite
become even more possible in tough times, but living from
these emotions cannot give you security or peace.

every time someone
loves themselves better,
builds their self-awareness,
understands their patterns,
improves their ability to communicate,
and expands their compassion for others,
the future of humanity grows brighter.
your healing impacts the world
by bringing in new peace.

give like earth
be flexible like water
protect yourself like fire
be boundless like air

where do we go from here? forward. the only way is forward. this journey has been long for the both of us. when it started, we were totally different people. we were full of hurt, we were confused, we were exhausted of being on what felt like an endless loop of sorrow. at some point it clicked in the both of us that life could be better, that it didn't need to be this hard, and that there had to be a healthier way to relate to the ups and downs. we searched, and we found our paths; we found our own ways to do the work. we used our effort to start chipping away at old patterns, to see things differently, and to finally lay to rest the past that we unconsciously carried. now we know that healing is possible, that change not only happens around us but also happens within us. we feel new, whole, yet still far away from perfect. if we are going to keep moving forward, and we have to because that is the only real option we have, we need to stop pushing ourselves to be perfect and just focus on putting one foot in front of the other; step by step we will get there. the place of our goals, the feeling of home, the feeling of success that we can give to ourselves only by fully accepting who we are. the world will keep changing, everything will keep changing, we will keep changing. but we will have our lessons, our memories, our peace, and this growing feeling of love for ourselves and all beings to help guide us. you and i need to remember that the point of all of this work was not to escape life or stop difficulty from ever happening again; it was actually the opposite: we taught ourselves to feel again so that we can embrace life. no matter how sweet, rough, or temporary it may be, let's promise ourselves to feel it all and to remember how fleeting it all really is.

sending love to all

about the author

diego perez was born in ecuador and immigrated to the united
states as a child. he grew up in boston and attended wesleyan
university. during a silent vipassana meditation course in
2012, he saw that real healing and liberation were possible.
he became more committed to his meditation practice while
living in new york city. the results he witnessed firsthand
moved him to describe his experiences in writing.

the pen name yung pueblo means "young people" and is meant
to convey that humanity is entering an era of remarkable
growth and healing, when many will expand their self-
awareness and release old burdens.

diego's online presence as yung pueblo, as well as his books,
inward, clarity & connection, and *lighter*, are meant to
serve those undertaking their own journey of personal
transformation.

today, diego resides with his wife in western massachusetts,
where they live quietly and meditate daily.

Andrews McMeel Publishing
a division of Andrews McMeel Universal
1130 Walnut Street, Kansas City, Missouri 64106

www.andrewsmcmeel.com

24 25 26 27 28 TEN 10 9 8 7 6 5 4 3 2 1

Paperback ISBN: 978-1-5248-7483-4
Hardcover ISBN: 978-1-5248-9515-0

Library of Congress Control Number: 2023939355

ATTENTION: SCHOOLS AND BUSINESSES
Andrews McMeel books are available at quantity discounts
with bulk purchase for educational, business, or sales
promotional use. For information, please e-mail the
Andrews McMeel Publishing Special Sales Department:
sales@amuniversal.com.

clarity &
connection

Also by yung pueblo

inward

clarity & connection

yung pueblo

Andrews McMeel
PUBLISHING®

contents

all human beings
are united by
birth,
life,
death, and
every emotion
in between

the biggest shift in your life happens when you
go *inward*.
you step in and observe all that you find with
acceptance;
the love you bring lights up your self-awareness;
you start seeing how the past is packed into your
mind and heart—
patience, honesty, and observation start the
healing process.

with time, intention, and good healing practices,
the past loses its power over your life.
you continue the process—stepping in, feeling,
understanding, and letting go.
and then you start noticing the results; you are
not the same anymore.
your mind feels lighter and develops a new,
sharper *clarity*.
you start arriving into your life and relationships
ready for deeper *connection*.

self-awareness

.

heal yourself, but don't rush
help people, but have boundaries
love others, but don't let them harm you
love yourself, but don't become egotistical
stay informed, but don't overwhelm yourself
embrace change, but keep pursuing your goals

next time you feel agitated
because you are falling back into past patterns,
remember that simply being aware
that you are repeating the past
is a sign of progress

self-awareness comes before
the leap forward in
your personal transformation

it is not easy

healing yourself
building new habits
observing reality without projection or delusion

this is work that takes effort

but if you persist
the fruits of your labor will
have an immensely positive
impact on your life

maturity
is knowing that
when your mood is down
you should not trust
the way you see yourself

throw away the idea
that healing is forgetting

the real result is no longer
reacting to old triggers
with the same intensity as before

the memories are still there,
but they do not have the
same power over your mind

i spent years unaware
that i was running away from myself,
always seeking company or entertainment
so that i would not have to face
the dark clouds storming inside of me

every moment was an opportunity for diversion;
friendships were a means of escape,
pleasure a temporary relief from pain

i did not notice that my relationships were shallow
because of how far away i was from myself

i did not understand why solitude felt unbearable
and why "fun" could not permanently settle
turbulent emotions

for far too long i was unaware
that the only way for life to improve,
for my relationships to feel rich,
and for my mind to finally experience ease
was for me to explore and embrace
the anxious unknown that dwelled within

you can change your location,
meet new people,
and still have the same old problems.

to truly change your life,
you need to look inward,
get to know and love yourself,
and heal the trauma and dense conditioning
in your mind.

this is how you get to the root.
internal changes
have a significant external impact.

i kept getting crushed
by my own expectations

barely present
thinking but not feeling
speaking but not listening
interacting but not noticing

smiling to continue the performance

my heart struggled with gratitude

never feeling satisfied
always missing what was in front of me

because my mind kept jumping
into imagining what more i could want

which made everything i was given
never quite as special as what i had envisioned

(disconnected)

after the trauma
i shifted into survival mode

unknowingly, i shielded my being with numbness

numb to letting others in
numb to my inner turmoil
numb to accepting what happened

unknowingly, i fell into a cycle of craving

craving safety
craving nourishment
craving no more pain

my reactions were large and loud
anything that did not go my way
was perceived as a potential threat

my focus centered on protecting
my delicate sense of self
i had little energy to place myself
in anyone else's shoes

it took the constant feeling
of dissatisfaction
and the exhaustion of never feeling
at ease
for me to start pulling myself out of my
dissociated way of living
and finally say "enough" to
a constant state of defense

(before awareness)

the friction
inside your mind
will keep overflowing
into your relationships

until you process
your emotional history
and understand how it shapes
your ego, perception, and reactions

do what is right for you.
do it over and over again.
lean into the light.

keep going even when it is hard.
especially when it is hard.

do not let doubt stop you.
trust the process when your mood is low.

let growth be your mission.
let healing be your reward.
let freedom be your goal.

everyone can benefit from self-healing;
even those who have not
experienced serious trauma
have at one point or another
felt the sting of heavy emotions

the mind feels these moments sharply
and they tend to ripple outward
impacting how we think, feel, and act

though we may learn to cope with mental tension
and the unexpected changes that cause turmoil

by taking a deeper look inward
we may be able to mend old hurt
and release old pain

by taking a deeper look inward
we may gain the courage to *evolve*

into greater mental clarity
into greater happiness
into greater patience
into greater honesty
into greater love

essentials to remember on tough days:

practice patience
accept what you feel
do not punish yourself
make sure you get good rest
give yourself ample kindness
accomplish smaller goals that day
do things that will calm your mind
a bad moment does not equal a bad life
struggle can be a space for deep growth
this current discomfort is not permanent

before you can see
someone else clearly
you must first be aware
that your mind will impulsively
filter what it sees through the lens
of your past conditioning and
present emotional state

sometimes you walk willingly into heartbreak
because it is clear that your time as partners
has run its course. for a while you fit together
seamlessly, but over time your paths have
started to diverge. it has become too hard to
meet each other in the middle and your heart
no longer feels at home. there is only so much
trying you can do before you say enough and
take a new direction. even though the future is
unclear, you know that moving forward alone
is what you need to grow and be free.

taking a moment
to figure out
how you really feel
instead of letting
old patterns decide for you
is one of the most
authentic things you can do

i have built a home with another person a few
times now, always expecting it to be a lasting
haven. as the storms came and went, the homes
would show their weakness and eventually come
apart. being left with the dread of sadness and
the hollow feeling of unwanted new beginnings,
it has finally dawned on me that if i build a
home within myself, a palace of peace created
with my own awareness and love, this can be the
refuge i have always been seeking.

sometimes a person ends a good relationship
because the areas they think are bad are being
intensified by their personal issues that they
have not dealt with properly. sometimes
people break apart a home because they
are unaware of their projections and are
not ready to appreciate a good thing.

heal yourself,
not just so you can thrive,
but to ensure that people
who cross your path in the future
are safer from harm

it is not easy, but the idea is simple:

the more we heal our own wounds, the less
likely we will be to cause intentional or
unintentional harm. perfection is not possible on
the interpersonal level. our individual perceptions
and changing emotions will occasionally cause
misunderstanding and accidental pain, but if we
can show up for each other compassionately, then
we can remedy the hurt that needs tending.

we often hand our tension over to others without
understanding that it wasn't ours to begin with.
someone passed it to us, and so we pass it to the
next person, and they to the next, until it lands in
the hands of someone with the tools to process it
and let it go. the more of us who are open to inner
work, the more points there will be in the giant web
of humanity where harm will not be able to spread.

the self-awareness needed to stop causing ourselves
and others harm is not just about knowing our own
inner mechanics, our trauma, the moments when
we are projecting, or how our reactions impact
our perceptions. it is also about taking the time to
understand what society has encoded in our minds
without our explicit permission.

radical honesty with ourselves is the starting point. it can help us overcome many complexes and help us see that there is much room for improvement. but to get to the root of the matter, to go even deeper, especially into the subconscious where many of our old patterns lie in wait, we need to find a practice that can help us process and unload this conditioning. we do not need to reinvent the wheel. there are already many proven practices that have helped thousands of people take real steps forward in their lives. our task is simply to search and find what works for us and then to commit to the inner journey.

when healing gets deep
there is sometimes
an explosion of emotion
that occurs to clear out
old energetic debris

you feel most agitated
right before you settle
into a more substantial peace

people are incredibly similar and different at the same time. we all have the same basic structure of mind and emotions, but we have distinct mental conditioning because no two people have experienced the same exact life. the twists and turns, the reactions we have felt, the things we have understood and misunderstood, all that we have come to believe, how we perceive ourselves and the world, the maze of patterns that impact our behavior, the different magnitudes of trauma—you can go on and on and see that each individual has their own inner world and unique emotional history.

since we are all so different, what helps one person heal may not help another person. what may seem too hard or too easy for some people may be a good fit for someone else or may be the right fit later on in life. fortunately, we live in a time when healing tools and practices are becoming more accessible. if we try, we can find something out there that meets our conditioning where it is at, something that we find challenging but not overwhelming, something that connects with our intuition, something that we are willing to spend time learning and practicing. there are so many options out there, from many different forms of meditation to a wide variety of therapy practices and many other healing modalities.

it is not about faking calm when

you actually feel turbulent emotions;
it is about accepting what has come up
without adding more tension to it

it is easier to trust people who recognize
when they have made a mistake
and are not afraid to apologize

this is a sign that they have
enough humility to be open to growth

a fresh start begins with forgiveness
and trust is greatly deepened when
changed behavior becomes consistent

neither of us knew
how to handle conflict
without making it worse

we never wanted to argue,
but it kept happening
because that is what hearts do
when they are overflowing with old pain

we did not mean the things we said;
they were just a reflection of the fire
that escalates when two imperfect people
compete to win

how many relationships would have
gone a different way if the goal were
not just to find harmony as a couple,
but to also find harmony
as individuals?

sometimes we wonder why it is taking so long to change and heal ourselves and why the same sort of heavy emotions keep coming up. we do not realize how rapidly we have accumulated patterns throughout our lives, especially during moments of intense emotion. after years of repeating the same behaviors, it takes time to change and adopt new responses to life. how many times have we felt anger, sadness, frustration, anxiety, and more? when we remember this cycle of repetition, it helps support our patience as we continue the process of letting go of the old, literally releasing remnants of the past during moments of deep healing.

one of the most important qualities
to develop in life is determination.

at some point you just have to
put your foot down and say,

"i am going to move in this
new direction and no person
or situation is going to stop me."

great transformations need a beginning.

a real conversation
free from projection
and ego-flexing
is a special gift

most do not talk to listen;
they talk to be heard

self-awareness, selflessness,
and a real desire to listen
are required for mutually authentic
and honest exchange

miscommunication and conflict occur because we are not building a bridge of understanding. often, in heated conversations, all we can think about is our own perspective, emotions, or ego. this limits our ability to empathize with the experience of another person, which is a prerequisite for the harmony that comes from understanding. one of the greatest gifts we can give each other is *selfless listening*, which is hearing someone's truth without projecting one's own emotion or story onto it—literally receiving another's perspective with complete acceptance.

in special moments, we can take turns deeply seeing one another. here we move beyond having an exchange into *holding space* while someone reveals their truth. this is a higher level of listening that involves acting as a compassionate audience for another person without interrupting or adding our own perspective. when we hold space for one another, hearts become more open, truth is ready to be revealed, and old tension comes to the surface so that it can be seen and held, not just by the speaker, but also the listener. this collective honoring of each other's truth can be incredibly healing.

i trust and feel at home around the ones who
are not afraid to be vulnerable with themselves,
who live confidently in their power and gentleness,
who try their best to live without harming others,
who are serious about their growth and healing,
and who have the humility to say, "i do not know."

it is okay to not have the answer

one of the bravest things
you can do
is boldly embrace the unknown,
accept your fear,
and continue to move forward

a clear mission
does not always have a clear path

how many times
has your mind
taken a small piece
of uncertain information
and spun a story around it that
ends up consuming your thoughts?

the mind is inclined to protect itself, but an attitude of defensiveness easily breeds anxiety. out of caution, we fixate on uncertain information and create stories that can lead to unnecessary fear and mental tension. taking a moment to notice when we are jumping to conclusions can save us from worry and grief.

through self-awareness, we can begin to notice when we are overthinking. the simple act of bringing our awareness out of the mental clutter of unreliable thoughts and back into the present moment can preserve our energy and decrease the friction we feel.

to be clear, there is nothing wrong with protecting oneself, but it is helpful to observe how often we take a defensive stance. if we are only ever defensive, we are surely getting in the way of our inner peace.

too many of us project our old conditioning
onto new situations. reactions happen
quickly and are based on past perceptions;
they make it challenging to process what
is happening in an unbiased and objective
manner. if you want to see things clearly,
use your self-awareness to intentionally set
the past aside and take in a fresh perspective.
redirecting your attention preserves your energy.

self-awareness is noticing
the rhythm of your thoughts

feeling when they are clear
and when they are out of sync

knowing when to take them seriously
and when to let them go

not every thought is valuable;
most are just the sounds of
impulsive emotional reactions

real maturity is observing your own
inner turbulence and pausing before
you project how you feel onto
what is happening around you

when you dislike what someone has done
and are quietly rolling in animosity toward
them, you are not only weighing yourself down;
you are strengthening future reactions of anger.
progress is realizing that fixating on what
happened cannot change the past, but a
calm mind can certainly help your future.

sometimes you need to move slowly
so you can then move powerfully

the modern world is so fast paced
that you feel the pressure to keep up

setting aside what everyone else is
doing and moving at your natural speed
will help you make better decisions
and lift up your inner peace

ask yourself:

is this how i actually feel, or
is this my emotional history
trying to recreate the past?

as our self-awareness deepens, we begin to
understand that much of who we are and how we
see the world is formed through the accumulation
of past emotional reactions. these moments of
intense feeling leave their mark on the subconscious
and predispose us to repeating certain behaviors.

the rapid movements of the mind are so subtle that
we can feel as though we are the makers of our
present destiny. in reality, the past is constantly
pushing itself into the present, inclining us toward
replicating old emotions and thoughts. the insistence
of our mental past gives us little room to decide for
ourselves how we actually want to feel. the past
does not take into account how things truly are.

the same way patterns accumulate, they can be
released. letting go is possible, but it requires
courage, effort, an effective healing technique, and
consistent practice. the mind is immensely vast; it
takes time to unbind old patterns that recreate the
past. when we begin to develop self-awareness and
a calm mind, the stories and patterns embedded in
our subconscious begin to surface for release.

when we travel inward, we may hit a particularly
rocky layer of the mind, a sediment of conditioning
that has been thickly reinforced. when we let go of
the hardened inner layers, we often feel the impact
of their release in our personal lives: the storms
of yesterday or the heaviness of past moments
rise to the surface. we may feel as though we're
on the edge of turbulence and disharmony as we
open ourselves up to deconditioning. real growth is
recognizing these moments and treating ourselves
gently as the storms pass.

to see your hidden patterns, you need to
intentionally build self-awareness. question
your perception, build a compassionate and
honest internal dialogue, dig deeper into
what your real motivations are, and have
the humility to know you can learn more.
self-awareness combined with action
opens the door to real change.

wisdom is accepting that there
are things you cannot force:

people change when they are ready

creativity moves at its own rhythm

healing does not have a time limit

love blooms when things align

unbinding

time does not heal all wounds; it just gives
them space to sink into the subconscious,
where they will continue to impact your emotions
and behavior. what heals is going inward,
loving yourself, accepting yourself, listening
to your needs, addressing your attachments
and emotional history, learning how to let go,
and following your intuition.

it sometimes feels as though time has helped us heal, but all it has really done is teach us to live with the wound. just because we have stopped thinking about the harm of the past does not mean it is fully healed. the passing of time allows what was first on a conscious level to sink deeper into the mind where it becomes a quiet yet powerful lever that forces us to behave a certain way. underneath our conscious thoughts remains the impact of a harmful yesterday.

healing requires moving inward with patience, honesty, and courage. if we do not address our accumulated subconscious patterns, they will simply remain there, always affecting how we think, speak, and act. our accumulated wounds and conditioning will restrict our flexibility and cause us to get stuck in a loop that continues repeating the past.

heartbreak is not always a sad ending;
sometimes it sets in motion a profound
transformation. it can open the door to truly
loving yourself, becoming more emotionally
mature, and learning what type of partner
would actually support your happiness.

letting go does not mean you have given
up, and it does not mean you no longer care.
it just means that you are releasing the
attachments of the past that get in
the way of your happiness and mental clarity.
letting go is the unbinding and disentangling
of old behavior patterns that pull you
into unnecessary mental tension and worry.
when you can be okay with things not having
gone a certain way, life begins again. making
peace with the past opens you up to love and
adventure and allows you to apply the lessons
you have learned with a new calmness.

many of us do not realize
how much we are actually suffering
until our awareness starts to expand

we do not see that our happiness has a ceiling
created by the sorrows and traumas
we have repeatedly suppressed

we do not realize that our reactions to life's
difficulties
stop us from seeing things clearly and place limits
on our ability to produce more creative solutions

we do not understand how powerfully our
past grips our present

so much of our internal struggle comes from not embracing change. tension decreases when we understand that change is happening at every level, from the atomic, to the biological, to the mental. a human being is composed of moving parts. our identity is no different. it is a dynamic phenomenon, similar to a river—flowing, moving, expanding, roaring, weaving, all the time with power and all the time with the potential to change. do not limit yourself to a static understanding of who you are. release your conditioned boundaries and be free.

may all of the times that someone
has made an incorrect assumption
about you activate a new sense of
humility and patience in your mind
that stops you from doing the same
thing to another person in the future

ask yourself:

is the connection real if there
is no space to be vulnerable?

the depth of our relationships is defined by
how freely we feel we can deliver our authentic
message. the deepest bonds are held together
by a bridge of honesty. real love holds space for
vulnerability, a place where we can be open, raw,
and even share parts of ourselves that are not fully
formed but are ready to be expressed.

whether within ourselves or in front of someone
who is close to us, vulnerability asks for non-
judgmental acceptance of our imperfections. this is
a form of compassion that can help us observe our
story in a different light, hopefully transforming
what was once burdensome into a more insightful
understanding. this is also a form of compassion
that allows us to accept the way things are without
trying to change it. sometimes vulnerability just
asks to be seen and heard.

if we are far away from ourselves, if we are
not honest with ourselves, and if we are full of
unexamined emotions and conditioning, we will
naturally find it difficult to be close to others. it
becomes easier to give loving support when we
have taken the time to explore our own inner world
and let go of the subconscious patterns that do not
align with how we want to show up for one another.

have you noticed that when
you feel the urge to change
someone, what you really want is
for them to behave more like you?

you cannot build a deep connection with someone
who is disconnected from themselves.

when we are in the habit of ignoring what we
feel or consistently run away from hard parts of
ourselves, distance is created not just between
us and ourselves but also between us and other
people. our lack of a full embrace of all that we are
can make our interactions with others superficial.
even if there is a desire to connect deeply with
someone, that connection will encounter limits
and will only ever reach a depth equal to the
relationship we have with ourselves. our personal
degree of self-awareness will reflect dimly or
brightly on whomever crosses our path.

if we can observe our emotions with open arms full
of compassion, it will be much easier to show up
and support others when they are going through a
moment of personal turbulence. if we can embrace
our own complexity, we will have patience as we
learn more about those closest to us. if we have
experience facing our own hard truths and being
present through our personal ups and downs, we
will have the emotional fortitude to wisely handle
challenging moments in a relationship without
immediately running away.

there is no other way to a life of fulfillment, happiness, and vibrant connections, but through thoroughly traveling the realms of our own heart and mind. areas that remain undiscovered are areas of potential friction that may manifest in our own mind or between us and the ones we love. all that is unexplored can show up as blocks that can stop the flow of harmony.

if we are accustomed to brave observation and practicing acceptance when inner turbulence tries to bring our attention to an unexplored or unloved part of ourselves, then the moments of friction within us or in our relationships will not become blocks. instead, these tough moments will become fertile ground to deepen our connection and refine our commitments. simply stated, putting the effort into knowing ourselves can only help us know others better. loving ourselves is essential if we want to live a good life.

when you feel agitated because you
think someone you love is not growing
quickly enough, remember that you had
to go slowly before you could make real
progress. managing your expectations and
knowing that people grow at their own speed
will save you from interrupting your peace.

attachment is not:

having desires, goals,
or personal preferences

attachment is:

the mental tension you feel when you do not
get exactly what you crave; it is refusing
to accept change or let go of control

when desire combines with tension, it morphs
into craving. attachment is when you start craving
things to be a certain way. craving is an extreme
form of desire that quickly attaches to different
ways of feeling and the objects/situations/
people that produce these feelings. attachment
is also when you try to place restrictions on the
unexpected and natural movements of reality. it is a
heightened form of the desire for control.

as the buddha put forth in his teaching, craving
itself gives birth to attachment. this dense form of
clinging to what we crave not only causes much
mental struggle, tension, and dissatisfaction, but it
also clouds our ability to objectively observe what
is happening within and around us.

wanting and craving are not the same thing. simply
wanting is a natural pursuit that focuses our energy.
craving occurs when wanting deepens and becomes
filled with tension or stress. the stress worsens when
we do not succeed in getting the thing we crave.

craving is ultimately the source of our mental
struggle and dissatisfaction. even when our
attachments are successful in molding reality,
we still find ourselves dissatisfied because craving
is an endless pit. once the sensation we pursued
has passed, the mind will return to craving more
because craving is what it knows best.

it is important to note that there is a substantial difference between craving and having goals or preferences. it is possible to pursue our aspirations without the stress that comes with craving and attachment. it is good and healthy to pursue our goals, but it serves us best to do so wisely and in a manner that does not make our happiness dependent on future achievements.

we know that something is a preference or a simple desire when we do not have the fate of our happiness connected to its realization. we know it is a preference when things do not happen the way we want them to and we accept this reality without the intensity of pain or hurt; we know something is an attachment when we feel mental tension, pain, and misery when we do not get what we crave.

sometimes the end is sudden
and you are left without closure,
heartbroken and unprepared
for such a sharp change

for a while, you live with a mind
that is half here and half full of regret,
wondering, "what if?"

for a while, your heart only feels grief
and your mind only sees gray

and then life starts to call you back
into its arena of possibility;
it reminds you that all is not lost
and that even though a chapter ended,
there is still a longer story to be told

with time and intention,
wounds lose their heaviness,
healing fills the tough parts of your being,
and you awaken the light of love within yourself

in time, you will return fully into the precious now
with a heart that feels refreshed and ready to move
forward

how many times has everything
come crashing down and left you feeling
as though the world was over?

now,
how many times
after grieving

have you gotten back up,
embraced the power of your determination,
and moved forward into a new life?

old patterns do not give up easily. they will try
to keep pulling you into reactions that lead into
repeating the past. but in time, after not feeding
them for a while and continually practicing your
ability to pause and respond, they weaken and
become easier to let go. they may still appear as
an option occasionally but will not have the same
strength as before. this is the turning point, the
shift that changes everything, the leap forward you
have been waiting for, the victory when it becomes
clear that you have moved beyond the past and
into a new life where you have matured enough to
intentionally be your own person.

learning how to breathe
and be okay
when my mind
feels dark and gray

to accept
this passing moment
without suppression
or lasting fear

to know that
the clouds moving through me
do not define who i am
or who i will be

learning the art of letting go
has been the skill my mind
has always sought

now i see that i am a river
always changing
while moving gently
in the direction of total liberty

they asked her,

"what is real happiness?"

she answered,

"happiness is not fulfilling every pleasure or
getting every outcome you desire. happiness
is being able to enjoy life with a peaceful mind
that is not constantly craving more. it is the
inner peace that comes with embracing change."

(being)

we often desire change in our lives, yet we reject
the changes that come about spontaneously. this
is a recipe that will repeatedly serve us misery. a
mind full of attachments craves the fulfillment of
its yearning and attempts to mold the world into the
shape it desires.

when we are controlled by our attachments, we
not only lose our peace of mind; we miss the
opportunity to enjoy life's natural unfolding. in
fact, all of the things we love and appreciate exist
because of continuous change. without change, life
itself would not be possible.

real happiness arises when we can love ourselves
and the world while welcoming and appreciating
change. this does not mean that we should live like
rocks and allow the river of change to flow around
us. love naturally motivates us to attempt to mold
the world in a way that enhances love, but wisdom
also teaches that we should not get attached to
things existing in an exact way, because change
will always come.

being okay with not being okay
does not make things
automatically better,

but it does stop you
from adding more tension
to an already difficult situation

being okay with not being okay
helps you let go

tough feelings and agitated thoughts cannot take
over your life when you meet them with ease,
acceptance, and a calm mind. sometimes these
old imprints bring with them visceral, rough
feelings that have been locked away but suddenly
have the space they need to momentarily arise
and evaporate. an important part of letting go is
feeling without reinforcing—you can be honest
with yourself about the heavy emotions that come
up and choose not to act them out or make them
worse. if you meet the rough parts of yourself with
gentleness, they will melt away, leaving you lighter
and giving you more space to act from a place of
wisdom. all you need to do is be okay with not
being okay during tense moments of release.

throw away the idea that you need to
pause your life until you are fully healed;
this is a different way of being attached
to perfection. progress happens when you
make better decisions in the midst of living.
you can simultaneously heal your past
while being open to the present.

how many times have you been
unable to fully enjoy a special
moment because you couldn't stop
thinking about what was missing?

when you are in an unavoidable situation
that is frustrating, treat your mental energy
like a precious resource. instead of fueling
your frustration with more agitation, which
will only make your mind more cluttered
and tired, realize that change will
eventually wipe all of this away.

many of our emotional reactions do not
have to do with what is currently going on.
they are actually old emotions accumulated
from the past—patterns that arise when
familiar situations appear.

the mind attempts to see the world in a way that
affirms its conditioning. our perception takes in the
present by categorizing and understanding what is
happening through its similarity to the past—this
creates a system of repetition that strengthens old
patterns. new events are normally not perceived
in their full clarity because their similarity to past
situations triggers old emotional reactions, which
quickly cloud the mind's ability to observe what
is happening objectively. we are seeing today and
simultaneously feeling all of our yesterdays.

when trauma becomes a part of your identity, it is harder to heal. the narratives that define how you see yourself need space to change. acknowledging your past is important, but so is doing the work to unbind those old patterns so you can move beyond them. allowing your sense of self to be fluid will support your happiness. change is always happening, especially within you.

expectations cause great misery for the individual.
we are constantly creating narratives of how
we want things to be and how we want others
around us to act. these narratives invariably
lead to disappointment because the stories we
crave are often dashed and broken by unrealistic
expectations, circumstances beyond our control,
and the randomness of the external world.

we forget that what unites all human beings is our
ignorance and room for improvement. we each
carry conditioning that clouds our perspective. our
time on earth is an opportunity to overcome mental
limitations such as unforgiving expectations and
a desire to control everything—limitations that
impede us from complete freedom and happiness.

as we do the work of examining our inner world,
it is unfair for others to expect us to be perfect and
for us to expect others to be perfect, especially
when "perfect" often means having others fulfill
our every desire. in a world full of imperfect
people, patience and forgiveness become essential.

it is easier to let go
of someone's opinion of you

when you understand
that others see you through
a combination of their past conditioning
and their current emotional state

without realizing it,
they see themselves first,
and through that lens they get
an unclear picture of you

there may be times when you
feel like a lot of what you've understood
no longer makes sense.

this might make you feel as though
you have regressed, but it is actually
a sign that you are opening new space for
deeper wisdom and greater perception.

when your previous understandings disintegrate,
they are not always immediately replaced by better
or deeper understandings. when you take your
growth seriously, you will often find yourself in
this in-between state;
it is okay to live without clear answers.

growth is not about forcing understanding;
it is about allowing it
to grow organically.

(shedding and expansion)

as you shed old programming and
your perspective expands, what you once
enjoyed may shift and situations that once
caused tension may no longer trouble you.
as your mind becomes clearer and lighter, the
world begins to look new. periods of integration,
in which you get to know yourself again, are
just as important as great leaps forward.

the world is a giant pool of moving vibrations,
waves of energy emitted from all beings.
when we cultivate our minds,
we cleanse our personal vibe.
we reclaim our power by
not yielding to what flows around us
and by allowing what is within us to come forward.
remember, the energy you most often repeat
is the energy you will most easily connect with.
your vibration is always shining
and affecting your environment.

reclaiming your power
is noticing when a story
based on assumptions
is making your mind tense
and intentionally bringing yourself back
to the present moment
as a way to cut the delusion

it is not about managing your
emotions; it is about managing
your reactions to your emotions

our reactions tell us what our mind has internalized from our past experiences. they are dense patterns that rise from the deep subconscious to protect us. this form of defense is not based on wisdom but on survival. when we start expanding our self-awareness, we begin to see that in moments of turbulence we have more effective options than repeating blind behaviors, which produce limited results that generally wipe away our clarity and inner peace.

we are not trying to control or manage the way we feel. we are trying to accept the shifts in our mood as the mind weaves through the large spectrum of emotions, moving from one emotion to the next, spending more time in some than others, but still traveling the whole human experience.

we immediately and unconsciously react to strong emotions. our reactions not only strengthen the emotion we are feeling; they imprint upon and accumulate within the subconscious, priming us to react similarly in the future.

we can manage our reactions, not by controlling what we feel, but by bringing awareness into the process. it is hard to change if you cannot see yourself. the light of awareness is especially useful when our reaction to a momentary emotion starts to undo our balance and mental clarity. our awareness lights up the darkness and helps us to see more options and information.

when we remember that emotions are impermanent just like everything else in this universe, it becomes easier for us to stand next to the river that is the human mind and watch as things flow by. self-awareness helps us overcome blind reactions that make already difficult situations more turbulent. without self-awareness, it is difficult to make choices that differ from those you have made in the past.

your initial reaction is usually your past
trying to impose itself on your present

know your sources of rejuvenation:

the amount of solitude you need to feel fresh again

the activities that strengthen your creativity

the people who light up your spirit

the love
between us

three thoughts:

relationships normally start with two people
wanting to treat each other well. harm is caused
when someone does not know how to properly
manage their reactions to their emotions. if you
think you *are* your emotions, then your words and
actions will resemble your mental turbulence.

in relationships, it is important to understand
that the other person cannot fix your emotional
problems. at best they can support you as you
uncover and process your own emotional history.

there is no such thing as a perfect relationship, but
there are incredible relationships in which the
mutual connection and support are indescribably
profound.

sometimes it takes your heart breaking
a few times for you to become independent
in important and healthy ways. heartbreak shows
you that your self-worth and wholeness should
not depend on another's words or love.
use the hurt as a map that leads
inward to pursue your healing
and ignite your self-love.

throw away the idea that you have to be fully
healed to be in a loving relationship with a great
partner. we normally come together with many
unresolved issues because healing simply takes
time. the couples who shine with harmony are the
ones who commit to healing and growing together.

vibrant relationships
feel like a sanctuary
where you are safe
to bring your vulnerability
and you are given ample love and care

a home
that equally supports
rest and growth
free from judgment
as you both seek to evolve

a union
void of control
but filled with
mutual understanding

it is easy to cause friction and unintentional harm
in a relationship when you do not know yourself
and have spent little time addressing your past
pain. how many relationships have folded under the
weight of unprocessed trauma, unhealthy patterns,
and unchecked reactions?

one of the toughest things
about relationships in which both partners
are open to inner growth
is when your partner uncovers
a thick layer of old conditioning or trauma
that they have to work through

you see them struggle and face the storm
but you cannot fix it for them

all you can do is hold space and
be ready to give them loving support

attributes of a good relationship:

selfless listening
calm communication
holding space for each other
strong trust, no need to control
authenticity, no need to perform
rest, laughter, and adventure together
the love between you is empowering
commitments to each other are clear
flexible, no need to always be together
both have the space to grow and change

attributes of a good friend:

they feel like home
they are honest with you
they remind you of your power
they support you in your healing
they have a revitalizing presence
they hold a vision of your success
they support you in new adventures
they lift you up with joy and laughter
they bring out the best version of you

friendships that feel like home are naturally
disarming. they remind us that we can stop the
performance and come forward the way we
authentically feel. the deepest bonds are spaces
where vulnerability is welcome. good friendships
have a reciprocal quality. when either person is
experiencing struggle, the other is ready to hold
space, to listen without judgment and with a
heart full of compassion. meaningful friendships
contain a bond that rises above competition. we
feel a friend's victory as if it were our own. true
sympathetic joy—the joy we feel for the success
of another—is the absence of jealousy.

friends who feel like family are rare.
when you are together, a timeless spark
lights up the path to joy, shared learning,
and rejuvenation. you seek to support
each other's happiness and naturally
rejoice in each other's success.

throw away the idea that you need to
find a perfect partner or a flawless friend.
all people are imperfect. what is possible
is connecting with someone who is doing
their own inner work. they will have more
practice with authenticity, holding space,
intentional growth, and self-awareness.

honesty
+
natural bond
+
laughter and joy
+
genuine mutual support
+
revitalizing interactions
+
authentic communication

=

empowering friendships

some of the biggest tests in life come when tough
things happen in your closest circle, when family
or friends who hold a piece of your heart go
through a struggle that you have no control over,
when all you can do is rise to the occasion by
listening to their words and radiating the love you
feel for them. though it is not for you to decide
how things will turn out, you can support, provide
comfort, and remind them that your love for them
is real and will remain unbroken.

some relationships do not have harmonious
beginnings. there is an undeniable pull that
brings the two together, but there is also
a distance between them created by their
unhealed hearts. this space within them,
filled with the unknown and unseen, causes
miscommunication between the two, friction,
and sometimes even unintentional pain. how
can they treat each other well when they
are still mysteries to themselves? the shift
comes when both commit to turning inward
to heal and know themselves. naturally, this
brings them closer together and elevates
the love and support they share.

conflict worsens when two people
fall into defensive reactions. then there
is no real communication happening,
only trauma arguing with trauma.

for real communication to happen, all projections need to cease. two people cannot see each other clearly and find common ground if both are thinking and speaking through dense clouds of emotion. so many relationships and friendships break because we do not have the tools and emotional maturity to see beyond our defensive reactions. when we notice our own defensiveness, pause, and come into a clearer thinking space, we have the opportunity for real conflict resolution. without vulnerability, patience, and self-awareness on both sides, there cannot be reconciliation.

without listening, honesty, and space for safe vulnerability, there is no communication. when we intentionally elevate the level of communication, the focus switches from telling someone how we believe they are, to clearly explaining our own perspective and how we feel. we can certainly share ways to better support each other, but first we need to accept each other's truth and move on from there. the support we ask for cannot be coercive; our partner needs to voluntarily commit to it for the union to be healthy.

blind loyalty does not nourish anyone

supporting those you love in their ignorance,
or even worse, continuously tolerating the harm
they cause you, is a serious act of self-betrayal

when you see your loved ones doing
wrong or walking into deeper darkness,
do not follow just because of
an old bond you may share

you do not need to sink together
you do not need to burn together
you do not need to crash together

even though it may be hard,
sometimes you have to listen to
your deepest sense of well-being
and go your own way to
preserve the good inside of you

maturity in a relationship is not expecting to always be on the same schedule. you are not always going to feel good at the same time. one may need more rest than the other, one may need more time to heal, one may pick up new habits more easily. people naturally grow, learn, and move at different speeds.

they asked her,

"what makes a relationship flourish?"

she answered,

"two people who seek to know, love, and heal
themselves as individuals will have harmony flow
between them as a couple. control creates tension,
but trust leaves space for individuality and opens
the door to vulnerability. calm communication,
clear commitments, and the willingness to support
each other's happiness make the union stronger."

(a vibrant partnership)

love is rejuvenated
when partners
occasionally ask each other,

"how can i better
support your happiness?"

a partner who supports your power is priceless;
someone who appreciates your opinions, who
has faith in your dreams and knows that you can
achieve great things. they recognize that you are
whole as an individual but are ready to complement
your life with their love and dedication. together,
you share the responsibility of leadership. with
gentle honesty and open communication, you
check in often to make sure you understand
each other well and are doing what you
can to strengthen your union.

a healthy relationship
is when two people equally take turns
being the one who steps up
when the other is going through
a turbulent moment

each is capable of listening
and holding space

each is self-aware enough
to check in with themselves
and not project onto the other

find a partner who is not afraid to grow.
if they are ready to notice their patterns,
let go of old conditioning, and expand their
perspective, then they will be ready to support
a vibrant relationship. two people who are
working on knowing and loving themselves
as individuals will naturally deepen their
love and understanding of each other. growth
comes with ups and downs, but it is also the
key to great harmony.

we walk through time together
holding hands
as the world changes
living in love
as we grow as individuals
meeting each other in the middle
as our youth gives way to maturity

loving people
does not mean
you let them hurt you

loving yourself and others
unconditionally
is a balance between
protecting yourself
and giving to others

find a partner who is as committed to
supporting you in good times as they are
in the tough moments of growth and healing.
coming together as imperfect people can be
challenging. imperfection can sometimes cause
unintentional conflict, especially when one is
going through a moment of inner turbulence.
patience, calm communication, and selfless
listening get couples through the storm.
conflict decreases when both turn inward
and focus on building self-awareness.

throw away the idea that your partner
can make you happy. they can be great
support, treat you well, and bring so many
good things into your life, but happiness
is only sustainable when it comes from within.
your perception, healing, growth, and
inner peace are your own to create.

find a partner who can appreciate your complexity. old conditioning from the past, behavior patterns, changing emotions, your true goals and guidance from your intuition—this flowing combination comes together to create who you are. when you focus on growing and letting go, there are many layers to unbind and shed. real love is finding a new harmony as you both evolve, taking the time to check in and find a new balance as your likes and dislikes align with your most recent growth.

real love is not always glamorous;
it is about being there when it counts
like when you have a tough day
and your partner sits quietly next to you
holding your hand
listening closely as you reveal
your worries
your inner struggles
and your brightest dreams

relationships take time to flourish. some people expect profound harmony immediately, but harmony is not possible without deep knowledge of one another's likes, dislikes, emotional history, and goals. the more you learn about each other, the more you refine your rhythm together. communication helps channel the love you feel for one another into clear ways of supporting each other's happiness. perfection is not an option, but you can undoubtedly build a great union in which you both feel safe, understood, and loved.

when an argument starts
your goal should be to arrive
at a mutual understanding

it helps to become aware of the inner tension
that is impacting your reasoning

notice your level of attachment
explain yourself clearly
listen with patience

find the balance between honoring your truth
and reflecting on your partner's perspective

and remember that success
is both of you feeling heard

maturity in a relationship is not expecting your
partner to constantly be happy. ups and downs
are natural. giving each other space to feel heavy
emotions while staying attentive and actively
supporting one another is a sign of real love.
relationships are not about fixing everything for
each other; they are about experiencing joyful
moments and tough times as a team and loving
each other through the changes. sometimes your
partner needs to go through their own process
to emerge lighter and freer than before.

how can we have a real conversation if every time we speak i can see in your eyes that my words are not reaching you? they stop at a narrative you have created about me based on who i was many years ago.

make deep connections, not deep attachments

with proximity comes the possibility for
connection. if we are in close contact with
someone, there is the potential for an intuitive
alignment to flourish. after spending a bit of time
with someone, we may desire to spend more time
with them. or we may simply be crossing paths.

as the connection deepens, so does the desire to
treat each other well. we go from being strangers
to becoming known supporters of each other's
happiness. even within families and friendships,
the bonds we experience are built on connection.
connection is based in the mind's innate ability
to love. however, the mind also contains a strong
drive to crave, which ends up conditioning our
perceptions of what we encounter and our reactions
to what we feel.

the deep connections that we feel toward our loved
ones are often wrapped up and mixed in with
attachments, not because we wish to make things
difficult, but because the mind has a strong tendency
to crave and control. attachments cloud the true love
that deep connections emanate. attachments create
much friction in relationships because they stand in
the way of individual freedom.

there is nothing wrong with wanting certain things
in a relationship, but we must resist coercing
others. instead we should build strong pathways
of honest and calm communication so that both
people can feel clearly understood. it is through
this mutually shared understanding that each
individual commits voluntarily to supporting the
harmony of the relationship.

a love without attachment is not a love without
commitment. attachments are attempts at
control marked by deep inner tension; voluntary
commitments are attempts at supporting happiness
and harmony marked by generosity.

base your relationship on clear communication
and voluntary commitments, not expectations

too often, we keep our expectations to ourselves
or we only partially hint at what we want. we do
not realize that we would be better off exploring
the ways we wish to be supported through clear
communication. when we are straightforward with
others about what we need to feel safe and loved,
we give them the opportunity to show up for us.

we are all different. even when we share a clear
connection that we can build on, we still need to
learn one another's likes, dislikes, strengths, past
emotional struggles, and reactive patterns.

communicating our needs, desires, and personal
emotional history gives both people the
information they need to better understand each
other and the opportunity to feel the natural
volition to commit and say, "these are the areas
where i can do my best to meet you. this is how
i can try my best to show up for you." in this
way, we transform our private expectations into
opportunities for commitment.

the difference here is subtle but important. there
is much greater harmony in a relationship when
neither party is attempting to be in control of it.
expectations are often attachments to shaping
outcomes, and they may leave one or both
partners feeling cornered and powerless. freedom
amongst people, in relationships and outside of
them, is based on understanding and voluntary
commitments, situations in which no one feels
pushed to be a certain way. when we transform our
expectations into opportunities for commitment,
we are cultivating freedom in our relationships.
even when clear communication and voluntary
commitments are practiced, we should still watch
out for manipulative behavior. the desire for
control can reappear in quiet ways, sometimes even
unconsciously. you know voluntary commitments
are being respected when you can freely say no to
a request without resistance, especially if it feels
outside of the bounds of your personal safety/
comfort/goals. every request will not be met with a
yes, especially when both partners are growing and
changing. in their essence, voluntary commitments
need to be optional.

there is nothing wrong with knowing what your
needs are in a relationship, but they are better met
when they are clearly communicated and when
*they match up with what someone is willing to
do for you out of their own desire to support you.*
when partners make commitments to each other of
their own volition, they create space for harmony
to flow abundantly in the relationship.

find a partner who can give you the space
you need to be your own person. it is healthy
to have different interests, likes, and dislikes.
you do not need to become the same person
to prove your love to each other. you know
you are both supporting each other's happiness
when each of you feels like you can be your truest
self. remember, trust blossoms in the absence
of control, and vibrant relationships should feel
like a balance of freedom and home.

your partner should accept you as you are
but also help you feel safe enough
to do the deep work of healing and growth

not because they want to change you
but because their presence energizes
and inspires you to flourish
into greater emotional maturity

it is not about finding perfection in another person;
it is about realizing when you come across
an undeniable connection that nourishes your
being and matches the type of support you are
looking for. getting lost in the idea of perfection
is a hindrance. when two people embrace their
imperfections and commit to growing into better
versions of themselves, they will naturally
experience greater happiness in the relationship.

find a partner who is willing to make clear commitments. you both know that supporting each other's happiness is not a mystery, it is the art of communication combined with action. what you need from each other will change over time. by building a culture of checking in regularly, your union will remain harmonious and vibrant. the way you love, trust, and show compassion for each other elevates your relationship into a space where you can both deepen your personal healing. true love does not fear change, it embraces new growth and adjusts accordingly.

having conversations without assumptions or
projections brings a couple closer together. taking
turns to really listen, using compassion to reflect
on the other person's perspective, intentionally
checking in with ourselves during the conversation
to see if we are being honest and clear—this makes
a difference and builds real harmony. when both
partners try to bring a high degree of presence
into their interactions with each other, it sets the
stage for true love to rise above discord and for
understanding to cool the fires of confusion.

it is not about finding a partner who
has flawless emotional maturity; it is
about finding someone who can match
your level of commitment—not just to
the relationship, but commitment to heal
themselves so they can love better, see
more clearly, and have more presence

find a partner you do not have to perform for.
when you are both committed to honesty and have
active compassion for each other, there is no need
to behave in ways that are not genuine. true love
is welcoming each other's changing emotions with
open arms. though you are both dedicated to
becoming the best versions of yourselves, you also
understand that not every day will be a good day
and not every step will be a step forward. being in
a relationship with a high degree of authenticity
and gentleness allows both partners to let down
their guards and feel at home.

the deepest friendships
reveal themselves during moments of crisis

when your world is shaken,
a friend stands and faces the storm with you

when things look dim,
they bring their light to remind you
that better days are coming

when you feel challenged,
they help you see your power

some friendships are so profound
that when you spend time together
it feels as though you have slipped
into another dimension:

a space where you both feel free and safe to
share the realest versions of yourselves,

a home where time stops and joy
shines without limits.

an irreplaceable friend is someone who:

highly values your trust
appreciates your honesty
naturally feels like family
still loves you as you change
finds it easy to laugh with you
holds space for you in tough times
supports your happiness and safety
helps you to believe in your self-worth
inspires you to love and know yourself

real maturity in a relationship is letting
your partner know when your mind feels
heavy before your thoughts find
a way to blame them for your tension;
openly naming that you are experiencing
turbulence allows you to know it is there
and your partner to know that it is time
to support you or hold space.

some friends hold a special place
in your story. they were there when
times were tough, they saw you clearly
when others did not, they believed in
you before you believed in yourself.
bonds that lift you up are precious
and easily go on to last a lifetime.

true love will accept you as you are but also
help you feel comfortable to shed the old and
transform into the greater you. many arrive
into a new relationship half-healed and half-
hurting. a mixture of thriving and surviving.
when the connection is genuine, supportive
of clear commitments, each person can start
to dig deeply into their individual healing, to
unfold and release the layers/stories that are
waiting deep within. progress in personal
healing ultimately elevates the mutual
joy of partnership.

growing

eventually you start to see changes.
your mind becomes light, the trees look
bright, the air you breathe begins to feel
like food for new opportunity, and life
takes on a crisp color pattern. ups and
downs will continue to come and there is
still much to learn, but you are calm now
and do not fear the old storms, which seem
to pass more quickly. a new awareness arises
to gently remind you that your power is
yours to wield and is ready to propel you
forward into peace and liberating insight.

be prepared to meet a new version
of yourself every time you shed another
layer of old trauma, conditioning, or hurt.
as you let go, your perspectives and interests
will shift. transformation is natural as you
travel the road to greater self-awareness,
happiness, and peace.

the goal is not to heal
and then begin your life.
the goal is to embrace healing
as a lifelong journey and allow
genuine connections
to emerge organically
along the way.

feeling emotionally exhausted is common
after opening up deeply or after experiencing
a series of heightened emotions for an extended
period of time. be prepared to take the quiet time
and solitude you need to fully rejuventate.
you are allowed to not be serious all of the time.

real courage is listening to your intuition
even when society and people in your life advise
against it

a lot of advice comes from fear,
people wishing you to stay with the herd
and do the normal thing

taking a calculated risk is not recklessness;
it is fearlessness

do not think in extremes; the answer is
rarely all or nothing. skillful action is finding
pathways even amidst contradictory options.
solutions are found by going beyond the
superficial and into the subtle. understand
that life is the integration of complexity.
everything is situational and multilinear.
find the middle path and challenge
yourself to think deeper.

give love, but don't exhaust yourself
be peaceful, but don't become passive
have patience, but don't settle for less
trust yourself, but don't develop arrogance
be open to love, but don't force a connection
have goals, but don't chase after each craving

when in doubt, remember you have:

the power to say no
the authenticity to be you
the patience to keep learning
the fortitude to continue trying
the courage to embrace change
the fearlessness to give selflessly
the wisdom to cultivate inner peace
the bravery to fulfill your aspirations
the openness that grows friendships
the awareness to follow your intuition
the intelligence to not repeat the past

they asked her,

"what does letting go mean?"

she answered,

"letting go does not mean erasing a memory or
ignoring the past; it is when you are no longer
reacting to the things that used to make you feel
tense and you are releasing the energy attached to
certain thoughts. it takes self-awareness, intentional
action, practice, and time. letting go is the act
of getting to know yourself so deeply that all
delusions fall away."

(presence)

it is not about expecting your partner
to make you happy; it is about clearly
communicating the best ways they
can support you as you travel inward
to ignite your own happiness

it is not possible to erase memories
or change the past, but you can stop
old behavioral patterns, decrease the
intensity of blind reactions, learn to
embrace change, accept all emotions
that come up, build self-awareness,
and strengthen good habits. healing
is intentional action plus time.

it is hard to see your progress
when you are deeply
immersed in the process

before you let doubt
take control

examine how much
you have grown and accomplished
by mentally taking a big step back
so you can look at the whole picture

we feel so safe with the ones we love
that we often share with them
our tension, our stress, our fear,
our sadness,
and even our anger

but let us remember to also
give them the best version of ourselves,
our joy and happiness, our excitement
and peace, our attention and care

gratitude makes you happy
attachment makes you struggle
gentleness reveals inner wisdom
harshness reveals inner turbulence
calmness supports good decisions
solitude supports transformation

essentials for growth:

proper rest
more learning
consistent honesty
building new habits
letting go of old stories
saying no to old patterns
believing that you can change
saying yes to supportive people
examining your emotional history
finding a practice to heal past pain
making time to build self-awareness

so often we spend our time living for tomorrow,
eagerly seeking results that can only come with the
slow buildup of consistent effort. especially in regard
to our own personal transformation, we forget that
building new ways of being does not come quickly
or with ease. a sturdy temple of peace with a strong
foundation that can withstand storms does not appear
overnight.

our anticipation of the future gets in the way of our
awareness of the present. a mind that is half in the
future is partially consumed in a dream—a dream
that can only become real through honoring what is
in front of us in the here and now.

every breath we take happens in the present. every
advancement in our growth happens in the present.
the wisdom that comes through feeling the truth of
nature can only accumulate within us through our
observation of the present. even when we rightfully
examine the past or plan for the future, the helpful
information we receive and integrate arrives to us in
the present.

when we set our goals, we set the stage for growth. from then on, in the moments that pass, we take opportunities to align our actions in a way that steers us in the direction of our aspirations. but if we do not honor and appreciate every small victory, if we do not feel gratitude for acting in the way that supports our transformation, then we will lack the practice to fully appreciate the accomplishment of our bigger goals.

remember, always craving specific results is a form of bondage that not only limits our progress but reinforces our inability to feel gratitude. the opposite of craving more is a gratitude that says "yes" and "thank you" to the present.

you do not need
a partner to feel whole
you do not need
to have everything figured out to feel successful
you do not need
to be fully healed to feel peace
you do not need
to be fully wise to feel happy

embracing yourself as you are
reinforces your worth and
decreases the friction in your mind

embracing ourselves as we are makes moving
forward into a better version of ourselves much
easier. sustainable personal growth requires
balance. if we hate who we are, it will slow the
work down—aversion increases mental friction.
while accepting where we are with radical honesty
can be difficult, as it can be hard to admit our
flaws, even to ourselves, it is the first important
step to real change.

if we can accept our imperfections and understand
that our conditioning limits our perception of
reality, this allows us to more easily begin the work
of undoing the past that is embedded in the mind.
there is a middle path where we can recognize the
characteristics that we want to develop without
adding the tension of aversion to our self-analysis.
embracing ourselves does not mean complacency;
it is the start of a journey into great mental clarity
and love for ourselves and all people.

one of the clearest signs of personal growth is
greater self-love, self-awareness, and love for all
people. inner work is not meant to turn us into
hermits or make us more self-centered. if we are
only reserving our kindness for ourselves, then
something is not right. if we are really trying
to grow our inner peace and wisdom, then our
capacity for empathy and compassion for others
will also grow.

inner work simultaneously makes us stronger
and increases our humility. we reclaim our power
and more easily follow our calling, but we also
recognize how fallible our perceptions can be and
how much more we have to learn.

when we go inward, we realize how much society
has conditioned us, created subtle shifts in our
preferences, and slowly formed our unconscious
biases. we think we are unbiased, but the record
of our past—meaning all interactions we have
experienced and all media we have consumed—is
always impacting our thoughts and actions. real
freedom is the ability to observe the world without
allowing our personal past to impose itself on what
we encounter. at their height, objectivity and selfless
love become one. practice makes a difference.

real friends know you have a range of expressions,
moods, and multiple aspects to your character

they embrace you as you are
and do not want you to perform

they know authenticity is not
being the same person over and over again;
it is allowing yourself to change
as you navigate life

heal at the pace
you know is right for you

what works for someone else
may not be what you need

each person holds
a unique emotional history

discomfort is part of growth,
but constant discomfort
is not healthy

self-love is balancing serious
inner work with rest and ease

slow moments are common
after a period of serious growth

they should not be feared
but embraced as opportunities
to get to know the new you

as you mature, you release so many layers
that you sometimes change radically,
and your mind and body feel like a new home

slow moments are for renewal
and integration of recent lessons learned

but a slow pace often finds a way
to test how you have grown;
this is an important time to observe your progress
and notice where you need further work

inner peace is not:

feeling perfect all of the time or
not caring about what is happening

inner peace is:

feeling and being with your emotions
without reacting to them; it is the calmness
that emerges when you embrace change

six things make inner peace easier:

not being afraid of change

kindness toward others

honesty with yourself

intentional actions

self-awareness

gratitude

life is difficult
and full of unexpected challenges

even so, you have to ask yourself:

how much stress and mental tension
are you unnecessarily causing yourself
by creating assumptions
and replaying fears in your mind?

how often are you refusing to let go
and adapt when things change?

how much of your inner turmoil
is self-imposed?

let's stop treating each other like machines.
it is okay if someone does not immediately
respond to your email. do not expect quick
replies to every text message. the internet
and social media have sharply increased
the demands on your personal energy.
be a human and take your time.

at a time when so many are striving to
get the attention of others, save yourself
the agitation by turning inward and igniting
your own self-worth. social media can be a
vehicle for inspiration or it can intensify your
insecurities. be mindful of how the content
you consume is impacting your emotions.

one of the hardest things about saying
no is potentially upsetting others. if you
know your path and what you need to focus
on, you have to be mindful of your limits.
save your energy so that you can accomplish
the goals at the top of your list. those attuned
to inner work will understand and respect
your right to say no.

for a few days i lost my way
and the past came roaring back

covering my eyes while old impulses
took their chance to reign over my mind

i let myself get caught
in the hurricane of yesterday

sampling my old home
remembering its walls and limits

feeling once again all of the reasons
why i decided to move on

the joy was empty
and what was once fun fell flat

i could not live comfortably in a home
too small for my recent expansion

i felt an immense wave of guilt
for taking a few steps back

but then it hit me
that reexperiencing
these old patterns and ways of being
was the motivation i needed
to finally close the door
and no longer feed the actions
that could only lead me in circles

they asked her,

"what is real freedom?"

she answered,

"freedom is mental clarity combined with inner
peace. freedom is when you can see without
projecting and when you can live without causing
yourself unnecessary mental tension or stress.
it exists whenever you are not craving more.
happiness and freedom are one."

(a clear mind)

check in with yourself occasionally
by asking these three questions:

is this the direction i want to be moving in?

are my recent choices helping my happiness?

what can i change to better support my goals?

practice the strengths of earth

have a giving nature
be grounded in your purpose
hold firm in times of turbulence

cultivate the qualities of water

move through life with gentleness
have access to your power at all times
flexibility and persistence increase success

embody the teachings of fire

transmute what you experience into light
be strong enough to have clear boundaries
have an awareness of when you need more fuel

internalize the values of air

release your expectations
embrace the constant movement of change
seeing is not everything; feeling is essential

(balance)

emotional maturity
is knowing the difference
between your true needs
and temporary cravings

your needs help you live
at an optimal level
and support your happiness

cravings are a reflection
of your agitation and attachments;
they leave you dissatisfied
and wanting more

overcomplicating your healing is something
to watch out for. you do not need to overthink
your past and repeatedly reimagine each trauma.
self-awareness has more to do with the present
moment—if you can see yourself clearly now,
you are more likely to act wisely. The best way
to access and heal your past is by not running
away from yourself in the present moment.

getting unsolicited advice is one of the best tests
and a great time to check in with yourself.

are they saying this for my benefit or their own?

does this advice connect with my intuition?

can i still treat them with patience and compassion
even if their advice felt unnecessary?

one of the hardest skills to master is
saying no to yourself so that you can
rise up and unfold into a greater you:

no to distractions or lack of consistency

no to the patterns and ways of being
that only lead back into the past

no to only doing what is easy

no to doubt and fear

a new life

power is visible in gentle movements

barriers bend and fall when we interact
with each other through an invitation
instead of a push

kindness has a disarming quality

because it carries a warmth that says,

"i am not interested in harming you"

take the risk

choose the direction you feel
burning in your intuition

life is a unique opportunity;
you can make best use of it
when you rise above fear

walking the uncommon path
is not a certain victory,
but it does provide the greatest
possibility for fulfillment

when she started letting go, her vision
became clearer. the present felt more
manageable and the future began to
look open and full of bright possibilities.
as she shed the tense energy of the
past, her power and creativity returned.
with a revitalized excitement, she
focused on building a new life in which
joy and freedom were abundant.

your relationships improve drastically and the
tension in your mind decreases significantly
when you can simply accept people for who
they are instead of fixating on how they
should change in order to be more
like you

six signs of maturity:

being open to vulnerability, learning, and letting go

seeing more perspectives than just your own

accepting responsibility for your happiness

prioritizing practices that help you grow

pausing to think instead of reacting

honesty with yourself and others

cultivate your humility
by questioning your perception
cultivate your humility
by not looking down on others
cultivate your humility
by not making assumptions
cultivate your humility
by being generous often
cultivate your humility
by learning from others

four teachers that give free lessons:

change

water

solitude

being

if i am always wanting
i have little time for being

only in being
can i feel real peace

maturity is feeling joy
for another's success

a mind trapped in competition,
one that feels a quiet bitterness
whenever someone gets a thing you crave,
is a sign that you are still at war with yourself

end the turmoil and friction by loving
and knowing yourself more deeply

even after healing significant trauma
and old conditioning, you will not be happy
all of the time. it is natural for your mood
to go up and down. what does change is
that you react less to old triggers and
when the mind feels turbulent you do
not fall easily into past patterns.

judging yourself by the first impulse
that pops up in your mind is unfair

that is just a copy of who you were in the past

what you intentionally decide to do
shapes who you are and influences who you will be
in the future

remember: pause, think, act

an honest and deep conversation with
a good friend is sometimes the exact
nourishment you need to regain clarity,
get back up, face the world, and resume
your mission with a new and focused energy

three signs of a good friend:

you do not have to perform for them

they hold space for you during struggles

they are truly happy for your success

progress is acknowledging where you are
and where you want to be without allowing
the space between the two to cause you
mental tension. if anything, it should inspire
you to continue moving forward peacefully
and diligently. having goals without attachments
produces faster results.

hurts travel through time

from one person to another
this unwanted heaviness moves
from the past into the present
and then into the future

one of the most heroic things
anyone can do is break the line of hurt

when people heal themselves,
they stop the hurt from multiplying
and their relationships become healthier

when people heal themselves,
they also heal the future

how people perceive you
is more reflective of
their inner mechanics
than your actions

you cannot control
how others think and live,
but you can be intentional
about the energy you put into the world

some may misunderstand you,
but what matters most is that you
understand you

real changes reveal themselves slowly. all this
work of letting go and building self-awareness
gives life a new, fresh feel. when you look out into
the world, you observe a reinvigorated vibrancy
that shines with the opportunity for a better life.
you use the power of choice, even when your
patterns try to pull you in an old direction. you
learn the value of accepting the emotions that come
up and being okay when you are not okay; this
allows moments of turbulence to pass quietly,
leaving your mind lighter and your eyes clearer.
you embrace a life of growth and the truth of
change so that inner peace can become your new
home.

happiness is being able to
enjoy the things you worked for
without slipping into
thinking about what is missing
or what you want next

saying no is a sign of progress
saying no is a sign of commitment
saying no is a sign of empowerment

saying no can help you fulfill your goals
saying no can support your mental health
saying no can bring you to the right people

in a world that is changing
and growing ever more rapidly,
inner calm is your most valuable asset

the type of calm that you can rely on
when there is turmoil around you

the type of calm that helps you
breathe deeply and make good decisions
when it is time for action

calmness helps the mind see clearly

comparison reinforces your anxiety

patience creates space for growth

anger ignites fear-based reactions

joy appears in the present moment

to release a grudge or a story
that is impacting your perception

remember that what you are seeing
is limited and cannot include the full
context of the situation

what you think happened is not final;
there is more to the story

it is not about having light
and kind thoughts all the time;
it is about not feeding the heavy
and mean thoughts. literally letting
them pass without allowing them to
take root and control your actions.

as we move into deeper wisdom, we become motivated by a growing sense of compassion for ourselves and others. it is easier to understand others and what drives their actions when we understand our own inner world.

as our conscious thinking evolves, we become gentler with ourselves and others. a new loving positivity emerges from releasing the tension of ego and allowing clarity to come forward—the essence of healing ourselves.

however, this gentleness and positivity should not be confused with a complete transformation. we can see signs of a new clarity emerging, but we must remember that the mind is vast, and the subconscious, where most of our emotional history is stored, holds much that still needs to be released. we are in a situation where our conscious thought patterns may have changed for the better, but our subconscious thoughts, the ones that sometimes spontaneously emerge, are still filled with the heaviness and harshness of old ways.

this is not to say that we should force ourselves to think a certain way or push down certain thoughts. we should just be aware that this lack of a linear trajectory is a natural part of the healing process and instead focus on cultivating the habits and practices that are helping us transform.

the thing about opening yourself up to healing
and growth is that, once some issues melt away,
deeper layers will have the space they need to
come up for observation and release. there is much
more accumulated in the subconscious than we
can initially comprehend. this is why letting go
is a long-term commitment. it is possible to get
to a much happier place while still working on
processing and undoing old patterns.

a strong self-love
helps you find a balance
between giving selflessly
and protecting yourself from harm

finding ourselves can lead to confusion
because who we are is always changing

finding ourselves can be complicated
without any deep healing

it is to our greater benefit to focus our efforts
on *freeing ourselves* from the burden of past pain
and patterns that do not serve our happiness

as we purify our being,
as we release the heaviness that dwells within,
everything about ourselves
and what we should do with our time becomes
clearer

our deepest aspirations become evident
the more we remove the dense clouds of ego
that wrap themselves around our consciousness

attachments are experts
at hiding in plain sight;
the mind may think it sees clearly
but its perceptions are often skewed.

only in the absence of ego
is there objective observation.
as "i" decreases,
wisdom is given space to be.

when you create something,
do not watch its progress
with attachment and anxiety

create it and let it go

give it to the world and let it be

feeling stressed over the outcome
and radiating vibrations of agitation
does not help you or your work

you know from your own growth
that real change is possible

even those who have caused much harm
contain this same dynamic potential

some may change more quickly than others
but the truth remains the same

with the right inner motivation
anyone can become
a better version of themselves

the future you will thank you for listening
to your intuition, for upholding boundaries that
supported your inner thriving, for saying no to
things that did not align with your values, for
taking the time to build your self-awareness,
and for staying true to your vision.

it is important
to understand yourself

but most of healing
is not an intellectual process

it is more about feeling
without trying to avoid

how we act is greatly impacted by the
subconscious patterns that control our
perception of reality

how we feel is deeply affected by our past
emotional history—heavy emotions that do their
best to recreate themselves in the present

what we see can only become objective
and clear when we observe, accept, and let go
of what was silently waiting deep within us

when we rise above the past and use our effort
to respond to life intentionally, by having the
perseverance to build wiser habits, we open
the door wider to living in a new way

the emotional discomfort we feel when we open
ourselves up to letting go is not always directly
connected to a particular tough or traumatic event.
much of our conditioning is generated in seemingly
small, everyday moments. reactions of jealousy,
anger, doubt, and low self-worth are easily
forgotten by the conscious mind, but they
can accumulate in the subconscious in a
way that primes us to feel them again.

in an era of uncertainty and unpredictability,
these qualities will make life easier:

a strong determination
a willingness to keep growing
the patience to listen to your intuition
the ability to adapt to unexpected changes
knowledge of what strengthens your inner peace
knowledge of your values and
the ability to stick to them

a successful life is created
with two words: "yes" and "no"

have the courage to say "yes"
only when it feels right

and "no" to the old patterns
that do not serve you

while your intentional actions
start to change
and your authentic feelings
begin to shift

your thoughts may need
some time to catch up with you

focus on being the more mature, more patient
"you" and old patterns will lose their strength

your thoughts will eventually align
becoming gentler and truer

do not expect perfection from yourself
even if you have done a great amount of
internal work

progress is acting intentionally
more often than you act blindly

and not punishing yourself
because you still have room to grow

allow mistakes to peacefully inform
your growth and learning process

you can tell humanity is maturing
because more of us are saying no to harm

we are taking time
to examine our biases,
moving our love from
being selective to unconditional
and expanding our idea
of what is possible

more of us are healing ourselves
and actively helping heal the world

in many ways, a human being is a microcosm of
the world. the conditioning that has accumulated
over time within the mind parallels the systems
that have become dominant within human society.
the reactive patterns of behavior that have been
repeated and reinforced throughout our lives as
individuals mirror the rigidity and slow change of
society at-large.

our minds are, in large part, the way they are
because of the countless defensive reactions we
have knowingly and unknowingly repeated. like
our minds, our world suffers from this pattern.
historically, people in positions of power have
tended to act blindly, allowing past fear and
trauma to inform their present.

as those who have delved into inner work know,
it takes time and self-awareness to break from
the past. it takes the repetition of positive and
nurturing behaviors that work against the flow of
ignorance and fear. more than anything, it takes
intentional action that arises from self-awareness
to break old habits that keep us from thriving. this
process happens at the collective level too. people
must think and feel together before they move
into action against systems of harm.

the importance of self-love and self-acceptance
in personal transformation work is critical. this
is the energy that allows us to embrace ourselves
completely and move forward with less friction
into healthier ways of living. similarly, humanity is
currently experiencing an expansion of compassion.
more individuals are recognizing that their love had
limits and are working to expand it to include all
people.

before healing takes place, the primary motivators
of most human beings are craving and aversion. the
accumulation of craving and aversion throughout
history has formed the society we know today. all of
this is held under a system of short-sighted, greed-
based economics that threatens our ability to live
well on our planet. collectively, we have not yet
learned how to accept our differences and treat them
without fear, nor have we stopped trying to change
and control each other. and we are still working on
thinking long-term.

working to grow in compassion and decrease the
hold craving and aversion have over our behaviors
is essential, but we must also deal directly with the
systems and ideologies of harm that have emerged
from these conditions. our task as people of the
twenty-first century is to embrace the complexity
that is inherent in the experience of the individual
and of humanity. if we can embrace ourselves
deeply and take action on behalf of ourselves
and all beings, we will be able to reorganize the
world into a place where all can safely flourish and
exercise their power.

people working on their healing,
the ones with new love in their hearts,
more self-awareness in their minds,
a greater ability to manage their reactions,
who are actively undoing their patterns and
biases, are helping to create a better world.
your compassion creates real change.

you may ask yourself: which comes first—inner
work or working to make the world a better
place? the answer is that both can happen at the
same time. we are all deeply imperfect and full of
conditioning that clouds the mind. inner work is a
lifelong journey, and so we should not wait until
we get to the "end" of our healing to help others.
practice your new habits and heal yourself while
you work to undo oppression on a larger scale.
moving against oppression is empathy becoming
one with action.

the inner work we do supports the larger movement
toward a better world. each makes the other
stronger. inner work helps us rise above our old
conditioning so that we decrease the harm we
recreate in our interactions. the outer work of
collective action makes compassion structural—it
helps us build a world where people can feel safe
and have their material needs met without directly
or indirectly harming one another. self-awareness
that becomes collective action is the medicine this
earth needs.

real communication happens when projections
cease and we are willing to listen to each other
in a selfless manner. this becomes more possible
when we engage with ourselves deeply, actively
work on healing our old pain and trauma, and
become familiar with our patterns. the more we
know ourselves, the better we can come to know
those around us. communication is critical to any
movement—it is how we focus our power and
collectively decide our direction.

three sources of hurt:

attachment

expectation

judgment

three sources of healing:

compassion

commitment

observation

part of knowing yourself
is taking the time to understand
the society in which you live

the direct and indirect messages
you absorb as you grow up
quietly enter the mind
and harden into conditioning
that affects your perspective

without knowing
you develop implicit biases

without critical analysis
the past takes root in your thinking

without awareness and love
it is hard to live compassionately

it is up to us to envision and enact a new standard
for society, to deeply realize the value of human life
so that the compassionate treatment of all people
becomes the guiding principle that dictates how we
design our communities, institutions, and nations.

our world has fallen into extremes. greed,
competition, individualism, and short-sighted
decision-making have created a world of plenty
for some and a world of struggle for most. we are
out of balance. we live within systems that push
against each other and easily cause direct and
indirect forms of harm. we do not yet know how to
win together or how to live well without damaging
our earth.

fortunately, humanity is in the process of maturing.
we are young, but we are more open to learning,
growing, and reorganizing our world than ever
before. *it is up to us to make compassion structural.*
to create an inclusive society in which people are
not left behind because of their differences but
embraced and centered so that all can flourish.

it is undeniable that we can improve our current global situation. to get to a better tomorrow, we must understand the complexity of today. the deeper our understanding, the clearer our actions. we must come to terms with history; face it directly without turning away. we must examine where the shadows of history produce present-day oppression. if we can accept the present reality of human experience, we can better position ourselves to undo structures that do not serve the common good.

the forces of racism and heteropatriarchy exist on the interpersonal and structural level. they impact our institutions and insidiously slow down the flow of compassion in our minds. we need to question our current economic system and support a greater distribution of material prosperity. none of our systems will last forever; nothing does. starvation, poverty, lack of access to good schooling and healthcare are structural problems that we can overcome—raising the standard so that people no longer suffer on the material level is not an impossibility; it is just a matter of will. collectively, we have the wealth and knowledge to accomplish this. what we are missing is a greater sense of unconditional compassion. society will never be perfect, but that should not stop us from making our shared reality more humane. when we commit to ending harm and supporting one another's thriving, all individuals benefit.

our task is to think and act more collectively
while supporting the freedom of the individual. to
standardize the humane treatment of all people.
to expand our idea of human rights to include
economic empowerment. to dream and act big. to
be the leaders we wish existed.

we have the power to reorganize the world and
make compassion structural.

imagine a world where love guides society

people would not be hungry or in danger
bodies would feel safe and minds fully nourished
voices would be heard and differences respected

disputes would be handled
without violence or terror
everyone would have access
to the things they need to flourish

sharing
listening
telling the truth
not harming each other
being kind to one another
cleaning up after ourselves

essential lessons we were taught as small children
would be taken to heart by adults and woven into a
new global culture

meet those you encounter with genuine
compassion. live with intentional gentleness.
cultivate peace with your hands and words. be
generous with your kindness. allow others to share
in the bounty of a heart that dedicates itself to
goodwill. these are marvels of the human spirit,
actions that are most easily taken by healed hearts.
not only do these ways of being help our minds
settle into inner peace, but they create safer spaces
in a world that is always moving in and out of
turmoil. to bring such goodness into the world will
benefit many and bring its own countless rewards.

it is to the benefit of your inner peace
not to harm others

let this truth settle into your mind
and awaken when things get tough

when you think
revenge will calm your heart
or erase the pain you have felt

remember

when you think
spreading the turmoil you feel
will ease the fire burning inside of you

remember

when you think
making life harder for someone else
will avenge your pain

remember

it is to the benefit of your inner peace
not to harm others

let this truth settle into your mind
and awaken when things get tough

sending love to all

about the author

diego perez was born in ecuador and immigrated
to the united states as a child. he grew up in
boston and attended wesleyan university. during
a silent vipassana meditation course in 2012, he
saw that real healing and liberation were possible.
he became more committed to his meditation
practice while living in new york city. the results
he witnessed firsthand moved him to describe his
experiences in writing.

the penname yung pueblo means "young people"
and is meant to convey that humanity is entering
an era of remarkable growth and healing, when
many will expand their self-awareness and release
old burdens.

diego's online presence as yung pueblo, as well as
his books, *inward* and *clarity & connection*, are
meant to serve those undertaking their own journey
of personal transformation.

today, diego resides in western massachusetts with
his wife, where they live quietly and meditate daily.

Andrews McMeel Publishing
a division of Andrews McMeel Universal
1130 Walnut Street, Kansas City, Missouri 64106

www.andrewsmcmeel.com

24 25 26 27 28 TEN 10 9 8 7 6 5 4 3 2 1

Paperback ISBN: 978-1-5248-6048-6
Hardcover ISBN: 978-1-5248-9514-3

Library of Congress Control Number: 2021931878

inward

inward

yung pueblo

Andrews McMeel
PUBLISHING®

two of the great lessons humanity
will learn in the 21st century will be:

to harm another is to harm oneself

when you heal yourself, you heal the world

reclaim your power,
heal yourself,
love yourself,
know yourself—
these phrases are becoming
more and more common. *why?*

because they are the pathways to
our own freedom and happiness

contents

distance

before i could release
the weight of my sadness
and pain, i first had
to honor its existence

i was never addicted
to one thing;
i was addicted to filling
a void
within myself
with things other
than my own love

to solely
attempt
to love others
without first loving yourself
is to build a home
without a strong foundation

three things make life harder:

not loving yourself
refusing to grow
not letting go

i lived so long
with a closed heart,
not because
i was afraid to get hurt
but because i was afraid
of the pain
i had hidden away

before we can
heal and let go,
what ails us
deeply
must first
come to the
surface

i spent so much time
creating versions of myself
that were far from the truth,
characters i would perform
depending on who was around

layers that could hide
the inner dance of turmoil,
between my lack of confidence,
the pain i did not understand,
and the uneasiness that comes
with reaching out to others for the
love that i was not giving myself

(before the healing)

i kept running away
from my darkness
until i understood
that in it i would
find my freedom

many of us walk the earth as strangers to ourselves,
not knowing what is true, why we feel what we feel,
actively working to repress experiences or ideas that are
too jarring for us to observe and release. it is a paradox
occurring in the human mind: we run away from what
we do not want to face, from what brings feelings of
pain, and from problems we don't have answers to,
but in our running away from ourselves we are also
running away from our own freedom.

it is through the observation of all that we are and
accepting what we observe with honesty and without
judgment that we can release the tension that creates
delusions in the mind and walls around the heart. this
is why the keys to our freedom lie in our darkness:
because when we observe our darkness by bringing our
light of awareness inward, the ego begins to dissipate
into nothingness and the subconscious slowly becomes
understood.

the mind is full of shadows, but shadows cannot
withstand the patience and perseverance of light—our
minds can become like stars, powerful united fields of
pure light. but unlike a star, the healed mind will dwell
in awareness and wisdom.

when we disconnect
from our pain
we stop growing

when we are dominated
by our pain
we stop growing

freedom is observing our pain
letting it go
and moving forward

(middle path)

it is not love
if all they want
from you
is to fulfill
their expectations

one of my greatest
mistakes
was believing
that another person
could hold together
all the pieces of me

make sure
the walls
you build
to protect yourself
do not become a prison

changes in the external world can cause great
misery when we do not know how to engage and
heal ourselves. moments of pain and discomfort, or
encounters with ideas that may break the mental
images we have created of the world, are normally
things we not only run away from but also things we
build walls to defend ourselves from. these walls we
build in our minds and hearts make sense when we
don't know any better. we all have the right to protect
ourselves from pain, but be aware that these walls
can turn from protection into prison—the more walls
we build around ourselves, the less space we have to
grow and be free. we have a harder time releasing the
habits that cause misery when we are surrounded by
the psychological walls we have constructed, causing us
to stagnate and fall into a rhythm where we are always
running within a space that is slowly growing smaller.

the opposite of this mode of being is to have a practice
that helps us go deep within ourselves to dissolve the
walls, to heal the patterns that cause us pain, to release
burdens and traumas, and to discover the universe
that dwells inside each of us. when we journey inward
and release the blocks that we first built as walls, we
naturally begin to create a new and wider space of
awareness. now when things happen in the external
world, we have more space and time to examine
how we would like to respond as opposed to reacting
blindly and reinforcing old patterns.

the body contains
our past emotions

healing work
creates space
for the release
of what we felt
long ago

don't run away
from heavy emotions

honor the anger;
give pain the space
it needs to breathe

this is how we let go

reminder:

when the body is tired
the mind will often create
worries to focus on

ask yourself often:

am i observing the situation
accurately or am i projecting how
i feel onto what is happening?

sometimes
we feel like exploding—
not because of anything
or to hurt anyone

but simply
because we are growing,
releasing,
letting the old parts die,
so that new habits,
new ways of being,
have space to live

(shedding)

yung pueblo

sometimes deeper mental clarity
is preceded by great internal storms

healing yourself can be messy

seeing yourself through honesty
can be jarring and tough; it can even
temporarily cause imbalance in your life

it is hard work to open yourself
up to release your burdens

like removing thorns from your body,
it may hurt at first, but it is
ultimately for your highest good

the dark clouds of rainfall are
necessary for new growth

an apology to past lovers:

i wasn't ready
to treat you well

i didn't know love
was meant to be selfless

i didn't know my pain
had control over my actions

i didn't know how far away
i was from myself
and how that distance
always kept us miles apart

(blind heart)

when passion
and attachment
come together,
they are often
confused for love

i spent most
of my life
trying to prove
to myself and others
that i had no pain
and felt no sorrow

some people hit rock bottom before
they change themselves drastically
because at that distance they can
best see who they really want to be

questions:

am i being honest with myself?

am i allowing myself the space to heal?

am i being compassionate and patient toward
myself when i am not meeting my goals as
quickly as i had intended?

am i doing what i need to do to thrive?

ego is
self-doubt
self-hatred
anxiety
narcissism
fear of others
harshness
impatience
a lack of compassion
and illusions

ego sees problems

consciousness sees solutions

ego is not just the idea that we are better and more important than others; it most often arises in the form of fear-driven emotions that grip our mind when we no longer believe ourselves capable of great things, when we look down on ourselves and treat ourselves harshly.

ego makes us see the world through fearful illusions; it makes us give the same punishing treatment we give ourselves to other people.

ego is a cloud that surrounds consciousness and disturbs its clarity. when we grow our self-love, our ego diminishes; when we purify ourselves and let go of mental burdens, the ego loses its power. as we learn to heal ourselves, we do not hate our ego, nor do we become complacent with the limitations it imposes on our lives. the highest happiness, the deepest sense of freedom, an unshakeable peace is possible when the ego no longer reigns, when the love of consciousness can flow without interruption.

the world itself is currently shifting from being ruled by the fear of ego to being liberated by the love of consciousness; what we face internally is a microcosm of what humanity faces globally—this is why growing our self-love is a medicine for our earth.

if you measure
the length
of your ego,
it will equal
the distance
between you
and your freedom

if you
are far away
from yourself,
how could
you ever be
close to another?

what is happening within us
will reveal itself in the energy
of our actions and words

honesty creates intimate connections
and decreases the turbulence of life

dishonesty creates distance and problems
that have to be dealt with in the future

if we are
not growing,
then we are
probably hurting

there is not a single moment when change is not
present. the constant of the universe, the motion of
impermanence, is observably evident in the world
around us and the world within us.

if we examine nature, it is clear that everything is in
a constant state of dynamic change. trees are a great
example: in cycles they alternate from experiences of
growth to experiences of releasing, all the while alive,
all the while growing. if we are refusing to grow, then
we are moving against the flow of nature; the flow
of change is so powerful that resisting it can only
cause difficulty.

sometimes growth hurts, but it is the type of pain
that is easier to endure because it is helping us come
forward as a better version of ourselves.

the greatest gift
sadness gave me
was the motivation
to transform

do not let a cloudy mind trick you
into doing things you are done with

reminder:

you can love people and
simultaneously not allow
them to harm you

the most widespread affliction
that people suffer from is a lack
of belief in their own power

to be so broken
to have
f a l l e n
so deeply
that the only thing
you can do is
r i s e
into a new you

(phoenix)

union

the healer
you have been
looking for
is your own courage
to know and love
yourself completely

it did not
happen overnight
and it was not
given to me by another

i am the maker
of the happiness and love
growing within me

make your growth
sustainable
by moving at a pace
that is challenging
but not overwhelming

there is a tendency to doubt
your growth in the midst of a
big leap forward; hold steady
and allow yourself to bloom

i do not wish
to change the past

it made me
who i am today

i only want
to learn from it
and live in a new way

letting go
doesn't mean forgetting;
it means we stop carrying
the energy of the past
into the present

healing begins with acceptance and culminates in
letting go.

when a great misery occurs, it remains with us for as
long as we hold on to it. attachments form because
of the energy we use to keep what happened, or the
image of what we want to happen, locked away within
our mind and body—this is the cause of tension in
our being. when we hold on to these attachments,
they travel with us as a burden, from our past, to our
present, and into our future. they can even be passed
on to our descendants long after we are gone.

the miracle of healing ourselves is so powerful,
because in the movement of accepting and letting go,
we relinquish the energy of burden not only in our
present but in our past and future as well. imagine the
time line of your life. now imagine the burdens that
you carry as an extra line layered on top. as we let go
of our miseries, this extra layer becomes thinner and
thinner. it will not change what happened, but the
extra energy we carried because of these occurrences
will no longer weigh down the time line of our life.
what happened, happened, but now these moments
are no longer attachments of pain and sorrow; now
they are experiences we learn from, lessons that bring
us into a present of greater freedom, happiness,
and wisdom.

when you grow rapidly
and experience
such deep insights
that you can no longer
look at yourself
or the world
in the same way

be kind
allow yourself
the time and space
to settle into the new you

(integrate)

let's make
s p a c e
for deep healing
in our world

a real sign
of progress
is when we no longer
punish ourselves
for our imperfections

you have
walked through fire
survived floods
and triumphed
over demons
remember this
the next time you doubt
your own power

she believed that the damage
to her mind and heart was permanent,
until she met wisdom, who taught her
that no pain or wound is eternal, that all
can be healed, and that love can grow
even in the toughest parts of her being

ask yourself:

is this worry real or is my mind just
looking for something to grab onto?

the mind is a series of patterns

if we wish to change ourselves
we should create new habits

when we build new habits
we are creating a new life

we carry
our attachments
and pain
in our bodies;
as we let them go
our bodies change

a body is a field of moving energy and a system of information. as life continues its fluctuations, we tend to gather attachments, burdens, and sorrows. we hold them so tightly that they become embedded in the body, causing blockages and disruptions in the flow of our system, which can limit access to the best possible version of ourselves—this sometimes manifests as ailments or disease as well as a lack of belief in our own power and a lack of understanding of the universe.

when we use purifying healing techniques, the body begins releasing these knots of attachment, allowing our field of energy to return to balance and move more freely and powerfully. this causes changes in our body: not just physical changes, such as the healing of disease or ailments, but immaterial and internal changes as well, such as believing in oneself more, the growth of love, and the aspiration to grow into wisdom. really, there is no separation between the mind and the body; they move together as one under the leadership of our mental contents.

if you spend too long not
letting yourself be creative
you can literally start feeling sick

you were born to create
let it flow, do not overthink it

i am not fully healed
i am not fully wise
i am still on my way
what matters is that
i am moving forward

i knew i was on the right path when
i started feeling peace in situations
where i would normally feel tension

find the tools you need to heal

every time i meet more of myself
i can know and love more of you

yung pueblo

a person
grows in beauty
whenever they
move away from
what harms them and
into their own power

never forget
the ones who
saw greatness
in you even in your
darkest moments

where do good decisions come from?
a calm mind

how can you measure your peace?
by how calm you stay during a storm

how do you know if you are attached to something?
because it creates tension in your mind

where are the greatest revolutions fought and won?
in the heart

do you know why you are powerful?
because you can change the future

feed your fire
cleanse your air
tend your earth
treat your water

(self-care)

progress
is when we
forgive ourselves
for taking so long
to treat our bodies
like a home

in one lifetime we can
be reborn many times

and so she moves forward,
with a little more wisdom,
a heart that is more open
to love, and a mind
that welcomes deep healing

(release)

i feel victorious
and free every moment
i do not measure my
personal value by
the things i do or own

a partner
who supports your dreams
and your healing
is a priceless gem,
a heaven in human form

(selfless love)

a hero
is one who heals
their own wounds
and then shows others
how to do the same

i started speaking
my truth
when being free
became more
important than guarding
the fear of my ego

her rebirth was stunning—
she lifted herself up from
the depths of despair,
grasped her dreams,
embedded them in her heart,
and walked forward into
a future that only her will
and vision could control

(revival)

i closed my eyes
to look inward
and found a universe
waiting to be explored

much of my confusion and sadness came from
being disconnected from myself. the greatest
journey i have taken so far is the one where i ended
the alienation between me and all that i am, the one
where i connected my light and my darkness, where
i united what i wanted to know with what i did not
want to face. only through this union and truthfulness
did i begin to feel at home within my own being.

(coming home)

forcing ourselves
to be happy is not
genuine or useful

being honest
about what we feel,
while remaining calm
and aware,
is the real work

reminder:

a sign of growth is being
okay with not being okay

there is an important difference between dwelling in misery and understanding that on the path of healing things will come up that sometimes cause us to feel the old emotions and patterns that we are working on letting go.

there is great power in honoring the reality of our current emotions—not feeding them or making them worse but simply recognizing that this is what has arisen in this present moment and that this will also change. when we create this space within ourselves—a space of calmness that is undisturbed by the storm—the storm tends to pass more quickly.

practicing such profound honesty within ourselves helps in all facets of internal and external life—there is no real freedom without honesty, and without honesty, there can be no peace of mind.

healing ourselves isn't about constantly feeling bliss; being attached to bliss is a bondage of its own. trying to force ourselves to be happy is counterproductive, because it suppresses the sometimes tough reality of the moment, pushing it back within the depths of our being, instead of allowing it to arise and release.

healing ourselves is the personal movement we embark
on to let go of all the conditioning that limits our
freedom; in this journey there will undoubtedly be
moments of bliss and difficulty. real happiness and
wisdom grow from the reality we experience, not from
the fleeting moments of bliss that we feel.

the more love
in my body,
the less harm
my body can do

who i am is always changing,
not because i am being fake
but because i am always open
to growth and transformation

it may have taken a long time,
but in the end it did not matter.
after much healing through
self-observation she now had
strength, she now had courage,
and the wisdom to wield her new
magic with virtue. no longer did
she run from her pain or her
troubles, no longer did she allow
delusions to capture her mind, no
longer did she doubt that the greatest
healer she has ever met is her own
unconditional love.

(you are a healer)

dear moon,

thank you for shedding light in the darkness,
for helping me know myself better than before, for
giving time and magic to the earth and order to our
nightly stars. you are a mother who sees all, knows all,
and asks for nothing in return.

i trust the ones
who are always
seeking to grow

the undeniable radiance of
someone who is not afraid
to grow, be free, and thrive

find someone you can heal with

i want a love that doesn't break
one that gives me water
when i am consumed by fire
one that offers me shelter
when i am lost
one that helps me see
that the hero
i am looking for
is me

(partners)

real love began when we
both stopped expecting and
instead focused on giving

many forms of modern-day love contain conditions, meaning that we have an idea that we want those we feel deeply for to fulfill. sometimes we don't see our hopes and expectations for the ones closest to us as conditional forms of love, because we perceive what we want for them as "good." unknowingly, in our wanting of what is "best" for them we limit our ability to give them the finest and most powerful form of love, a selfless love that empowers them to decide for themselves what is best for their lives.

so much of what we think is love is actually attachment and expectation. focusing on giving in our relationships isn't easy; it is a habit that requires strengthening, repetition, healing our minds, and allowing our selfless nature to come forward for it to become our new normal. there is a special harmony that arises when two people focus on giving more to each other, a subtle communication and growing awareness between them that allows for better support of each other's happiness.

we may worry, "how will i ensure that what i desire is met?" a better question may be, "has solely focusing on meeting my desires truly brought me happiness?" the happiest people, the ones who have successfully purified their minds of all conditioning and craving, tend to have such a strong compassion and understanding of love that their lives naturally focus on giving to others. in this giving and clarity of mind they find happiness.

though most of us are far from having fully liberated
minds, it is always worth understanding that giving is
one of the most powerful forces we can set in motion,
that through giving we not only support those around
us but also wisely follow the law of nature—everything
we do will ultimately come back to us in some form
or another. if everyone focuses on giving, we will each
receive more.

they were wrong.
this pain, this heartache,
these harmful habits,
they don't last forever

why? because the heart
is made of water and
the mind is made of fire—
the essence of both is change

the will to heal can remove
the deepest stains on our spirit

progress is being aware when there
is a storm happening inside of you
and remaining calm as it passes by

what does it mean to "live in love"?

it means to rise above judgment so that we may see the
world and ourselves with eyes of compassion. it means
allowing the wisdom of love to orchestrate our actions,
to always seek to produce thoughtful movements that
support the good of all beings, and to emit peace into
the ocean of humanity with our every step. living in
love is allowing ourselves to move through life with
an open heart so that all may share in the gift of our
goodwill and kindness. it is to ask ourselves, "how
would love heal this situation?" before we make
our move.

i want to live in a world where harm
is not systemic, where love organizes
society, where the earth is respected,
and where life is valued above all else

anyone who is willing
to know themselves,
to face themselves with
honesty and work toward
loving themselves and
all beings without condition,
is a hero who is adding to the
collective peace of humanity

two things are true:

people who truly know and love themselves
cannot be hateful toward other people

the same way we are anchored and grounded
by the earth, the earth is healed and nurtured
by our unconditional love

a human is as deep as an ocean,
yet most of us spend our lives
knowing only the surface

when we decide to dive deep
within ourselves, we set in motion
the miracle of personal evolution

(deeper healing)

though the pain
once felt unbearable
and everlasting,
the peace i feel today
is a testament to the
heart's ability to heal

all along i have searched for
knowledge when what i was
really looking for was wisdom

not the information that fills
my mind with details and facts

but the experiences that fill
my being with freedom,
healing, and the light of insight

(liberation)

then came the day
when i looked into a mirror
and saw ten thousand faces;
in that moment i understood
that my body not only holds
a multitude of stories
but that i also exist
in many places
and many times
at once

(timeless)

rebirth:

the moment people
wake up to their power
and start moving
toward their freedom

my mission
is to heal
my mind
with wisdom
and to infuse
my body
with love

allow yourself to transform
as many times as you need
to be fully happy and free

the inward movement can be summarized as follows:
we observe ourselves, we accept what we find without
judgment, we let it go, and the actual release causes
our transformation.

we are already always changing, but when we focus
on healing, we can change in the direction of our
choosing; these are moments when we intentionally
reclaim our power. every moment we take to know
ourselves, we return as someone new.

whatever calms and concentrates the mind causes the
purifying release of old burdens that weigh us down.
one can be successful with simple inward observation,
but when we observe ourselves through proven healing
techniques, including different forms of meditation and
practices of yoga asanas, among many other things, we
accelerate the process of change.

different techniques reach different levels of the mind.
ultimately, any practice that you feel is challenging but
not overwhelming and is giving you real results is the
right one for you at the moment. as we progress, we
may take on sharper tools for deeper healing. anything
that can heal the subconscious of our mind and create
space for love is powerful enough to completely change
our lives.

when things get tough, remember that we are not building something small, we are building a palace of peace within our own hearts. it takes determination and effort to complete something of such beauty and magnitude.

when you want to change yourself, do not change everything at once. pick a few things to focus on first. setting yourself up for success is key.

trying to change too many things at once is sometimes overwhelming. being consistent with a few changes, applying them in your life until they become integrated as new positive habits, helps you build a strong foundation for future transformations. setting yourself up for victory helps you build momentum; it makes the consistency required to achieve greater goals in the future much more attainable.

goal:

find the balance
between being
productive and
being patient

letting go is medicine
that heals the heart

letting go is a habit
that requires practice

letting go is best done
through feeling, not thinking

heaviness comes from hanging on tightly to emotions
that were always meant to be ephemeral. it is not easy
to let go, especially when all we know is attachment.
we want things to last forever and we turn difficult
moments into long-lasting pain simply because we
have not learned to let go. we have not learned that
the beauty of living comes from the movement of
change. letting go does not mean that we forget, and
it does not mean that we give up. it just means that we
are not letting our present happiness be determined by
things that happened in the past or by things we wish
to happen in the future.

there is no mystery to
the miracle of self-healing;
it is courage, commitment,
and consistency that move us
from misery to inner peace

i gathered my habits
and started releasing
the ones that can
never lead me to
lasting freedom and joy

i am making more time for the
people who make me want to
be the best version of myself

as her love grew, her ability to feel the
unseen and listen to the wisdom of the
eternal strengthened. the walk on the path
to freedom had changed her; though she
still experienced times of difficult release,
the feeling of unity remained ever present
in her body. now that she lived her life in
the grassy field between mortality and the
infinite, she could feel that the space in
her heart was the same as the heart of
the earth and the heart of the universe.

(awareness)

~~thank you for making me happy~~

thank you for supporting my happiness

i am
at my
strongest
when
i am calm

it is the things
you say no to
that really show
your commitment
to your growth

when chaos is all around you
the wisest choice is to create
peace within you

your peace shines outward
and supports the creation
of a new harmony

(meditation)

we live in a unique time, when fear-driven and hateful
emotions are coming to the surface so that they can be
completely released, so that we can create a new world
where institutionalized forms of harm are no longer
factors in our lives. as it works for the individual, it
also works for the collective of humanity—we can't
heal what is ignored, nor can we live happily and freely
if we continue running away from our own darkness.

personally, my faith is in people. our courage to
turn inward in the hope of uncovering and releasing
all that stands in our way of becoming beings of
unconditional love is what will bring harmony and
peace to our world. unity with those around us is most
possible when we become internally whole and loving.
wisdom more easily flows through us when our minds
and hearts are no longer reacting to the suffering of
everyday life. this does not mean that we will become
cold or distant; it means that we will learn to respond
calmly to the inevitable changes of life without causing
ourselves misery. we will learn to respond to life as
opposed to blindly reacting to it.

humans affect one another deeply, in ways that the
world at large is just beginning to understand. when we

begin healing ourselves, it sets off waves that connect
us to those who have healed in the past and those
who will heal in the future. when we heal ourselves,
it gives strength to those who need more support to
take on their own personal healing journey. what we
do reverberates throughout time and space—like a rock
thrown into a lake, the circles it creates move in
all directions.

as she looked into her past,
she noticed that the road
she had traveled was
no simple straight line.
her journey toward fully
loving herself and the world
was full of forward and
backward movement,
twists, turns, detours,
and even some pauses.
at times, she doubted her progress,
her potential, and even
her power to change.
but today, with the
wisdom of experience at hand,
she knows she could not have gotten
to where she is without every
movement she has ever made.

(experience)

serious transformations begin
with two commitments:

the *courage* to try new
things and act in new ways

the *honesty* needed to no longer
hide from or lie to ourselves

the people
with the power
to move and act through
unconditional love
will be the healers and heroes
of our planet

(a new balance)

interlude

there was a woman who lived in a small town near a
tall mountain. she had lived in her beloved town all
her life. everyone in the community thought highly of
her and appreciated her kindness and calm manner.
she lived a quiet life and worked as any other
normal person.

those close to her knew that she was a dedicated
meditator, that she sat silently for a few hours a day
in deep self-observation. when they would ask her why
she took meditation so seriously, she would simply
respond by saying, "i like to learn and peace
is important to me."

as time went by, her calmness continued to grow and a
saintly radiance became apparent in her eyes—but only
a few were aware that a great change had happened
within her. a day came when she told those closest to
her that she would soon be leaving the town to live by
herself near the top of the mountain. when asked why
she was leaving, she merely stated, "it is time for me to
fully unlock my freedom." some tried to dissuade her,
but most trusted her and felt comfort knowing that the
mountain was close by.

a decade quickly and quietly passed. the people began
thinking of her as their guardian angel because ever
since she had moved up the mountain, the town had
become calmer and more prosperous; they imagined
that it might be from the good energy that she
regularly emitted.

there was a group of young people in the town who
had vague memories of this woman who was slowly
becoming a living legend. they were curious and
hungry for wisdom from someone who had become a
being of complete freedom. it had somehow become
common knowledge that she had accomplished this
goal. none of them had seen her since they were
children, but they heard stories from people who would
occasionally venture up the mountain to visit her.
those who saw her would return to the town inspired
and rejuvenated.

one day the young people gathered their courage
and decided that it was time to pay her a visit. they
organized their questions, packed light bags for a short
trip, and made their way to the mountain in hopes of
sharing in the woman's clarity.

the following are a few of the questions and answers
between the young people and the one who is free.

they asked her,

"how did you free yourself?"

she answered,

"by embracing my own power."

they asked her,

"what does it mean to love yourself?"

she answered,

"it means to uncover and release whatever keeps you
from true happiness; to love, honor, and accept every
single part of you, especially those that are kept in
the dark. it means to observe yourself continually
with the utmost honesty and without judgment. loving
yourself means striving to reach new heights of self-
understanding so as to cultivate the wisdom that inner
peace requires."

they asked her,

"what is the key to saving the world?"

she answered,

"you. you are the key. heal yourself, know yourself,
make yourself whole and free. release all limits so that
your love can flow unconditionally for yourself and the
world. this will open the heaven of your heart and it
will guide you without fail."

they asked her,

"why are we here at a time when
there is so much misery and despair?"

she responded,

"because you answered the call. the earth signaled for
heroes, and the heavens sent forth the ones who were
most ready to grow and unleash their unconditional
love. you're here to shine the light of your own
healing, to offer the world the gift of your balance
and peace."

they asked her,

"are you wealthy?"

she responded,

"yes. it took years to build, but now there
is a palace in my heart that i have constructed
out of awareness, calmness, and wisdom."

they asked her,

"what is true power?"

she answered,

"true power is living the realization that you are your
own healer, hero, and leader. it is when you share your
truth with compassion and peace. your power grows
when you make progress in your own freedom and
wisdom. those who are truly powerful do not harm
themselves or others; instead, they use their energy to
enrich all they know with love."

self-love

self-love
is the beginning:
an essential centerpiece
that opens the door
to unconditional love
for yourself and all beings

self-love is a sincere
acceptance of the past

an agreement to make
the most of the present

and a willingness to allow
the best to occur in the future

(wholehearted)

self-love
is the nourishment
that gives us
the clarity and strength
to love others well

self-love is personal evolution in action

being honest
with yourself
is an act of
self-love

self-love
is creating space
in your life to heal
your body and mind

do not confuse self-love
with thinking that you're
better than everyone else

true self-love is accepting
yourself for all that you are,
especially the darkest parts

the more we love ourselves, the more easily
prosperity and miracles can flow into our lives

self-love has the power to release all blocks

through self-love we can travel the universe

self-love is doing the work
we need to do to be free

self-love begins with the acceptance of where we are now and the history we carry, but it does not stop there. self-love is an energy we use for our own personal evolution; it is a meeting and balance of two critically important ideas: loving who we currently are and simultaneously transforming into the ideal version of ourselves. though these ideas may seem contradictory, they are both required for our ultimate success. without acceptance, our transformation into a happier and freer self would be highly difficult. why? because it is much harder to change and let go of what we hate.

self-love helps us delve deeply into ourselves and release the patterns in our subconscious that impact our behavior and emotions. true self-love is when one understands that the inward journey is the path to freedom, that observing and releasing our inner burdens is what will make us feel lighter and more aware. self-love does not grow the ego; it does the opposite. it is our ego that carries the craving that causes our suffering—the incessant craving that rests at the center of the ego is the ultimate block that stops us from achieving freedom.

since true self-love
is the gateway
to unconditional love
for all beings,
this must mean
that many people
in our world are suffering
from a lack of self-love

(the missing peace)

your
self-love
is a
medicine
for the earth

as your self-love
grows stronger,
so do the waves
of change that
you can create

the beauty
of self-love
is that it can
grow into the
unconditional love
that can end all harm

with self-love, we have the determination and
courage to move deeply inward using honesty as
our guide. this inward movement transforms our
being, dramatically enhancing our awareness of who
we are, our understanding of the universe, and our
capabilities as individuals. a beautiful result of this
process is that our new sense of compassion toward
ourselves does not end with us; it blossoms and flows
outward into the lives of others and has the capacity,
if consistently cultivated, to encompass all beings.

this growing compassion becomes the centerpiece
and active component of a love that knows no
limits. unconditional love for ourselves and others
completely respects our sovereignty as individuals
and honors our power by no longer allowing
ourselves to be harmed by anyone. this limitless love
also gives us new grace and clarity that help us see
ourselves in all other beings and better understand
where they are coming from. it gives us the strength
to treat all with kindness and support all in living
lives in which they are no longer harmed.

unconditional love can bring balance to our world.
the clarity it produces can help us better understand
the roots of harm and work to eliminate them so
that all can have the external freedom needed to
work on their own internal liberation. the greed
and reactiveness that cause harm can be replaced
with love as the primary motivator and responses of
kindness as our principal form of action. to create

this shift in our world, many will have to heal
themselves deeply by doing their inner work, releasing
burdens within themselves, and creating enough space
so that their own self-love can breathe deeply and
expand into unconditional love.

as more expand into this field of greater egolessness,
the world will shift with us and be significantly relieved
of the greed that sits at the center of the imbalance
that we currently experience. our love as a humanity
does not need to be perfectly unconditional to change
the world—every time our collective love grows, it
creates a better future.

understanding

healing yourself will ask more of you

more rest
more self-love
more letting go
more time for learning
more space for transformation
more honesty about how you feel
more time developing good habits
more courage to try new practices
more faith in yourself and the process
more time cultivating your inner peace

things to practice and integrate:

unconditional self-acceptance
not harming yourself or others
patience without complacency
giving without wanting

i cannot
make you happy,
but i can
commit to support you
in the creation
of your own happiness

to expect another to resolve all of our issues and give us the happiness we desire is to expect to see the sunrise without opening our own eyes. it is to ask a river to give us nourishment without dipping our own hands into the water. another cannot answer a riddle that was only ever meant for our own minds to solve. the universe seeks to enlighten and empower us, thus it is only rational that we are our own greatest healers.

happiness may seem elusive. try as we might, no matter our external setup, happiness will come and go. the sea of life flows between calmness and storms. either something outside of us will cause us some sort of struggle or something from within us will arise that is asking to be acknowledged and released. a human being is an accumulation of aversions and cravings, which periodically rise from the depths of our mind so that we can have the opportunity to let them go. why? because our nature is not to be full of burdens; we are meant to be light, free, open to the harmony of love and the wisdom of the universe.

though happiness will come and go, we do have the power to deepen our experience of it and extend our time partaking in its heavenly nature. to do so requires effort on our part to enhance our relationship with ourselves so that we may discover all that impedes our contentment and release it from our being.

while in the midst
of serious internal growth
respect your need to rest

love is not:

i will give this to you
if you do this for me

love is:

i will give this to you
so that you may shine

true love does not hurt; attachments do

love cannot cause pain; attachments cause pain. we
create attachments in our mind when we want to
hold on to something or someone, or when we expect
things to be a certain way. when the attachments that
we create in our minds break, we feel their rupture
deeply. how deeply depends on how much we identify
with the image that we have created. when things
happen contrary to these images that we hold dear in
our minds, we feel pain from these attachments being
stretched and broken.

attachments are not a form of true love. unconditional
love, selfless love, a love without expectations is a
higher form of existence that creates no attachments
or images. it is a state of profound egolessness.
expectations and judgments are attachments that
the untrained mind repeatedly creates, causing more
knots and burdens that impede our happiness. the
typical human mind is eclipsed by the delusion of ego;
the ego separates, categorizes, and labels everything
that it comes across, causing our discontent and
misunderstanding.

all mental tension comes from not letting go

stress and anxiety are the children of
attachment; they are both forms of craving
that take us away from the present and into
areas of imagination that steal away our peace.

wanting always interrupts being

peace makes you strong
hate reveals your emptiness
kindness feeds your happiness
anger reveals your fear
love makes you free

how to lead yourself:

1. develop a relationship with your intuition

2. have the courage to follow its guidance

i can only
give to you
what i have already
given to myself

i can only
understand
the world as much as
i understand myself

as she was swimming in the ocean of wisdom
that dwells in her heart, she understood deeply
that all was a part of her, that no one was
separate from her. she whispered lightly with
newfound peace, "i am everything." that was
when she realized that her greatest power is,
and always was, her ability to love herself.

wholeness
is when lies
no longer stand
between you
and yourself

how to improve your life:

1. make self-love a top priority

2. learn a self-healing technique

3. create space for daily healing

4. know that everything changes

5. be kind, loving, and honest to all

i am not
here to
compete

i am here
to grow
and be free

every time we compete with others, we are already
losing, because we are forgetting that life is not a
race to be won but a journey we embark on to build
our inner peace and wisdom. we create nonexistent
competitions in our minds when we get carried away
by the delusions of ego. the hierarchical conditioning
of society combined with our attachment to "i," "me,"
and "my" creates a scenario in which only a few
can succeed.

having a world built on competition has created
a situation in which humanity is overflowing with
misery—we thought we had to win, to harm each other
to survive, but the moment we submitted ourselves to
this scenario, we took a step away from our individual
and collective freedom.

releasing these conditioned habits is difficult but
essential, because happiness and internal security
grow as we release the "i" of ego and the delusion
of competition. the wisdom of love shows us that
individual and collective life need to be reborn and
reorganized in a way that supports the well-being of
all, not the few. love teaches us that we are here not
to compete but to support each other's growth
and happiness.

unconditional love sees no one as an enemy

my faith
for a better future
is in the people
who are turning the idea
of unconditional love
into a way of life

if you want to know
how free you are,
ask yourself,
"how far does
my love extend?"

there is a path
we can walk
where we no longer
allow anyone to harm us
while also loving
all beings unconditionally

fear seeks control
revenge prolongs pain
animosity disrupts peace
compassion ignites healing
honesty releases burdens
happiness is letting go

loneliness
will not
go away
if we remain
far away
from ourselves

repeat daily:

notice the stories you hold in your mind

let go of the ones that cause tension

sometimes people are simply meant to
teach you how not to act in the future

everyone is a teacher, but that does not mean everyone is correct.

there have been times in our lives when we have been a good example for those around us, while at other times we have not been a good example. if we recognize our own imperfections, it helps us have compassion for all people and look upon all as equals.

just because someone was wrong once, it doesn't mean they are going to be wrong forever. similarly, just because we may perceive someone as wrong, it does not necessarily mean that we are right. in most cases we lack the perfect information required to form an objective and universal perspective.

it is important to remember that we are all imperfect and that we all live through the limited perspective of ego.

striving to learn as much as we can from one another without making harsh and permanent judgments is a sign of wisdom.

part of
being human
is having
opportunities
to give and
receive forgiveness

i am not sure when i will
be completely free and healed,
but i do know i will feel it
more clearly than anything else
i have ever felt in my life

she's an explorer,
unafraid to travel
within her heart and mind,
ready to discover new spaces
to heal—releasing burdens
and planting wisdom wherever
her awareness takes her

the strongest
people
i have met
are the ones
who do not
harm themselves

the idea that
when you let go
of what you want,
it comes to you

working toward our goal and simultaneously letting it
go may seem paradoxical, but it is the fastest way to
achieve what we want. letting go is not giving up; it
is the graceful walk between continuing to put effort
into making our preferred reality come true and not
allowing our happiness to be controlled by something
we do not have. if we remain attached, we tend to feel
agitation or even misery. this creates tension in our
being that blocks us from fulfilling our desires.

sometimes we may still get what we want, even if we
do not know how to let go; but in these cases, we may
be less capable of keeping what we want, and it may
even cause us more misery because we never addressed
the root of our tension, which is our inability to
appreciate what we already had to begin with.

what do we get when we let go of the past and the
future? inner peace. realizing peace within ourselves
no matter our external circumstance is a high form
of freedom that allows blessings, miracles, and success
to flow into our lives. happiness and gratitude are
attractive forces; their lack of wanting is what clears the
road so that new things may come with greater ease.

water teaches flexibility and power
earth expresses firmness and balance
air sings of intelligence and bravery
fire speaks of action and growth

the mind
is a garden;
what we decide
to grow there will
determine our prosperity

bad vibes
can't hurt you
when your balance
and love are strong

sometimes
we go back and repeat
an old mistake
just so we can remember
why we moved forward

giving yourself
the space and time
to respond
instead of reacting blindly
is an important way
to reclaim your power

the body knows what it requires;
listen to it—not the cravings of
the mind but the needs of the body—
let it guide you into well-being

(intuitive healing)

your friends
who have the courage
to expand their
wisdom and self-awareness—
they are special;
keep them close

the forces
of the universe
support those
who work at
healing themselves

peaceful minds
have the power
to create
a peaceful world

when the mind feels wild and cloudy,
it may be that something from deep within
has come to the surface, an old burden
seeking release. *breathe, relax, and let it go.*

(storms)

sanity is the unwillingness to do harm

i held my fear by the hand,
honored its existence, and
thanked it for teaching me
that happiness exists beyond
the boundaries it creates

free
people
have no
masters
but themselves

movements change the world, but just as it is
important to be a part of and build movements to
create a world where human rights are a reality
for all—a world where systemic forms of social
and economic oppression no longer exist—so it is
equally important to build our own intimate internal
movement that focuses on healing the greed, hatred,
and fear within ourselves that cause so much chaos
in our lives and are the actual underlying roots of the
societal chaos we experience.

every society is simply a composition of its individuals
believing, consenting to, and perpetuating particular
stories that come together to create the world we
know. if the stories we choose to believe in change, if
we begin to understand that when we harm another we
are actually harming ourselves—not in a fictional sense
but in a literal sense, similar to the way that water is
good for the body and poison is bad—then we will
quickly shift into a new world.

pleasure cannot fill the heart
hate cannot keep you safe
anger cannot set you free
only love can fill voids
only love can create peace
only love can liberate

love
is the most
potent and versatile
form of magic

love
is the strongest
building material
in the universe

not just
the love
between people
but the love
that gives you
the power
to heal yourself
and change the world

they both know that they are not together
to complete each other, that their happiness is
their own to create. nevertheless, their ethereal bond
serves a great purpose; it gives them the time and space
to love each other well enough to release the tension of
their unloved hearts. their love for one another is not
the end but rather a means to an end. it is a humble
tool of healing and nourishment that can strengthen
their minds and make their spirits mighty, so that they
may both travel as far within themselves as possible,
so that they may both release all that limits the flow of
their happiness, so that they may both swim freely in
the waters of wisdom and universal understanding.

(love is a key)

"'strength'? what do you mean by 'strength'?"

"what i mean is how firm is your inner peace,
how honestly can you observe yourself without
judgment, how limitless is your love for yourself
and all beings, and how willing are you to change
yourself for the better?"

courage
+
letting go
+
self-love
=
a growing awareness

as our ability to
know and heal ourselves
deepens, we will be better
equipped to examine the
world more carefully
and heal it more
effectively

healing yourself with love
is a long-term process

healing the world with love
is a long-term process

i rebel by loving more

whenever we are asked to limit our love, to be selective
with our love, to reserve our love for some parts of
ourselves and not others or to reserve our love for
some people and not others, we do a disservice to
ourselves by following along, because any love withheld
becomes tension in our being.

the normality of perpetual war, the rising tide of
poverty, the varying forms of violence our economy
requires to stay afloat, and the indifference that we
are expected to feel toward it all are stifling and ever
present. when we think of happiness, it is important
to remember that, generally speaking, we fall together
and we rise together. those of us alive today have never
lived in a world where a large portion of humanity was
not struggling to meet its material needs or fighting for
the right to be treated as human beings—we humans
have the uncanny ability, whether we are aware of it or
not, to feel and be affected by the plight and struggle
of others. energy sees no barriers.

whenever we are asked to keep our eyes and hearts
closed, and we do just that, because it is easier
than accepting the responsibility of a world and
humanity that need healing, because it is easier than
understanding that to heal the world will require a
heroic effort on our part to heal our own inner world,
we are dimming the light of our own future. it is in
the challenge of allowing our love to flow actively and
limitlessly that we come to find greater degrees

of our own personal liberation and global liberation for all beings.

the dalai lama once stated, "compassion is the radicalism of our time." this is true. today we rebel by loving more. when we can see and treat each other as family, we will know a global peace.

do not forget
to send your love
into the earth
into the water
into the sky

how will you help heal the world?

by healing myself and supporting
the healing of those around me.
by allowing love to fill my very
being and guide my every action.
by understanding that if it causes
harm, it must not be the right way.

observe.

accept.

release.

transform.

because being calm in the midst
of chaos is a sign of true power

measure
your success
by the growth
of your freedom

the mind is a lot more vast than conscious thought
can comprehend. the conscious part of the mind—the
part where we feel and hear the movements of our
emotions, memories, and thoughts—may seem large,
but it is quite small in comparison to the subconscious.
an iceberg's small peak floats above water while the
great majority of its mass sits silently and unseen
underneath—the top is visible and prominent, but what
is unseen is much bigger and has a massive effect on
the part that is seen, largely dictating its movements.
the mind works in a similar manner; the subconscious
and the reactive patterns that have accumulated there
over time, though they remain mostly unknown or
forgotten, have a strong effect on our daily behavior.

this is why there is a lot more to freedom than simply
having unrestricted mobility or having our material
needs met or the removal of all forms of external
oppression. freedom is deeper than believing that
we are free on the conscious level of the mind—
the conscious may think this to be so, but if the
subconscious is still burdened with patterns that cause
us misery, delusion, and the pain that comes with
unceasing reactions, then we are not yet wholly free.
the greatest oppressor is the untrained mind.

freedom grows when we begin the mental healing and
training that teaches us how to let go and interact with
the ocean of life in a way that no longer causes us
misery; our freedom grows as we observe deep within

ourselves and begin letting go of our attachments and
burdens that clog up the subconscious mind. freedom
is happening every moment when we are not craving
something more.

the mind is purified as we release the weight of the
past and the yearnings for specific things in the
future—especially if our happiness is dependent on
obtaining these things. the mind is clear, powerful,
and effectively decisive when we can truly observe
the present moment without projecting our ego onto
it. freedom is something we build within. freedom
is a habit.

~~find yourself~~
free yourself

goals:

develop my calmness
cultivate my wisdom
expand my freedom
help heal the world

releasing,
learning,
expanding—
i am happily a
work in progress

sending love to all beings
may all beings continue reclaiming their power
may all beings heal themselves and the world
may all beings be happy and free

about the author

diego perez is the writer behind the pen name yung
pueblo. the name yung pueblo means "young people."
it serves to remind him of his ecuadorian roots, his
experiences in activism, and that the collective of
humanity is in the midst of important growth. his
favorite word, "liberation," took on a deeper meaning
once he started meditating vipassana, as taught by
s.n. goenka. through writing and speaking, he aims to
support the healing of the individual, realizing that
when we release our personal burdens, we contribute
to a global peace.

Andrews McMeel Publishing
a division of Andrews McMeel Universal
1130 Walnut Street, Kansas City, Missouri 64106

www.andrewsmcmeel.com

24 25 26 27 28 TEN 10 9 8 7 6 5 4 3 2 1

Paperback ISBN: 978-1-4494-9575-6
Hardcover ISBN: 978-1-5428-9378-1

Library of Congress Control Number: 2018942082

ATTENTION: SCHOOLS AND BUSINESSES
Andrews McMeel books are available at quantity discounts
with bulk purchase for educational, business, or sales
promotional use. For information, please e-mail the
Andrews McMeel Publishing Special Sales Department:
sales@amuniversal.com.